NAJDA
in
NEW YORK CITY

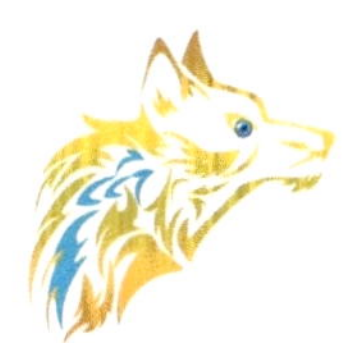

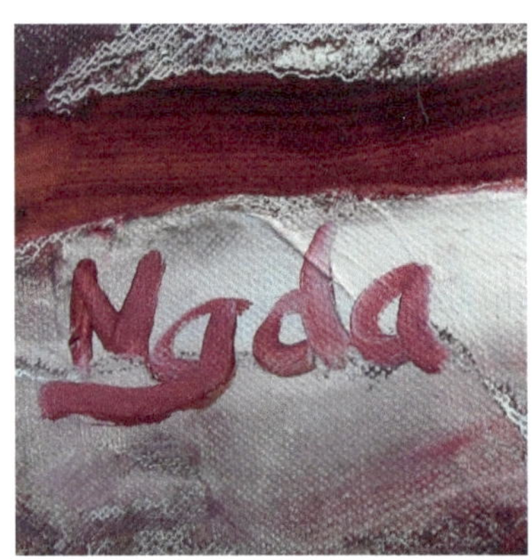

On the cover:
"Man With Skull, Woman with child and
the tumbleweed of life in the middle"

Painting technique: Oil painting on Canvas
Size: 70 cm x 100 cm
Year: 2015

*** * ***

Layout Cover and Internal by: Wolf Graham

ISBN 978-1-911424-71-0

Publishing Company:
Black Wolf Edition & Publishing Ltd.
4 Begg Road, Glasgow G40 2AA Scotland
www.blackwolfedition.com

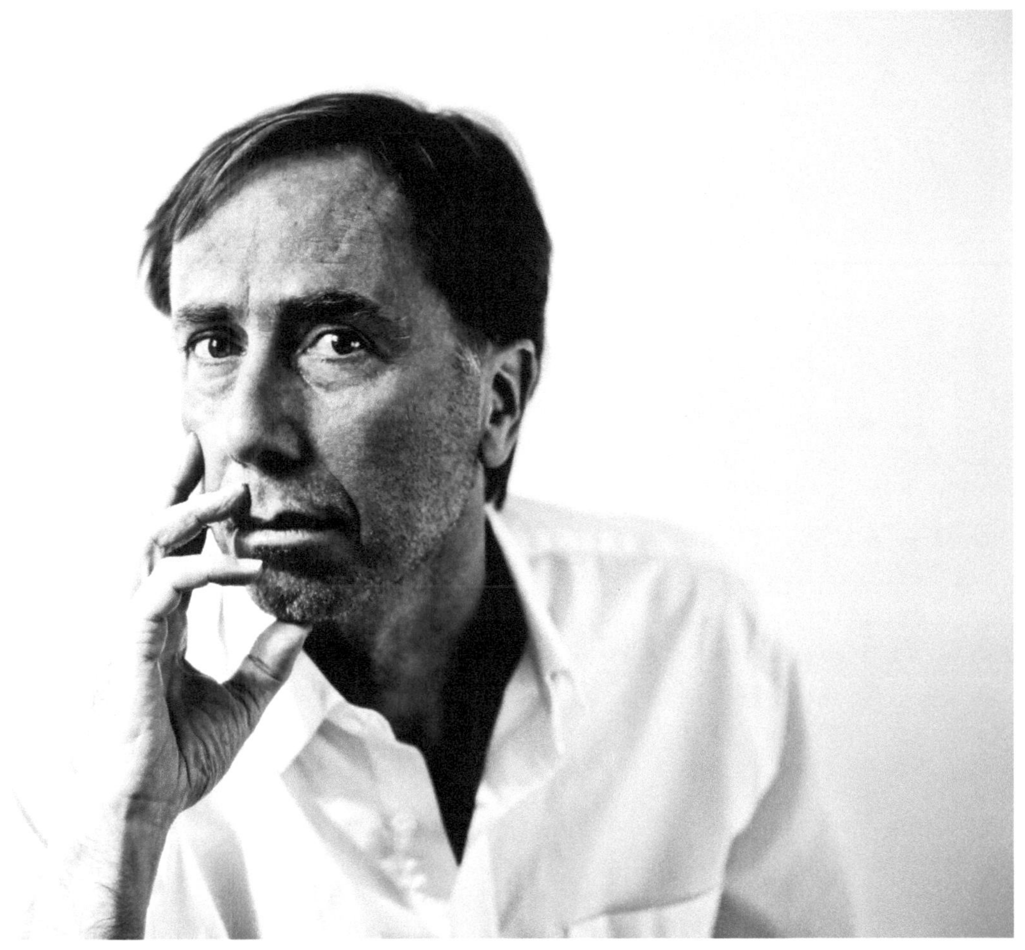

Was born in a Glasgow tenement of Scottish-Polish parentage. The Scottish mountains were an early lure. Since then, Stephen has climbed extensively in the wilderness mountain areas of Europe, the Middle-East, Africa, Asia and the Americas.
Stephen graduated with a PhD in physics from St. Andrews University. Followed by research posts in physics at Tokyo University, CNRS Grenoble and Oxford. Stephen returned to Glasgow to work with a photonics high-tech company and has been 're-born' in Poland with another high-tech venture.
Stephen discovered art by chance and good fortune, pre-empting a 'new path' of discovery and self-expression. Najda's art spans the complete spectrum of human emotion from simple beauty of sensual curvaceous women; through captured moments from the artist's travels; through a wide range of scientific, social, political, philosophical and intellectual questions and debates; to the provocative and challenging brutal reality of war, disease and human tragedy. These theoretical concepts are brought into focus through the medium of oil on canvas to create a unique visual experience. The art is both, wonderful and enlightening, pleasurable and challenging, beautiful and harrowing, complex and terrifying, producing powerfully evocative images that are entirely relevant to the modern world and questioning our path into the future.

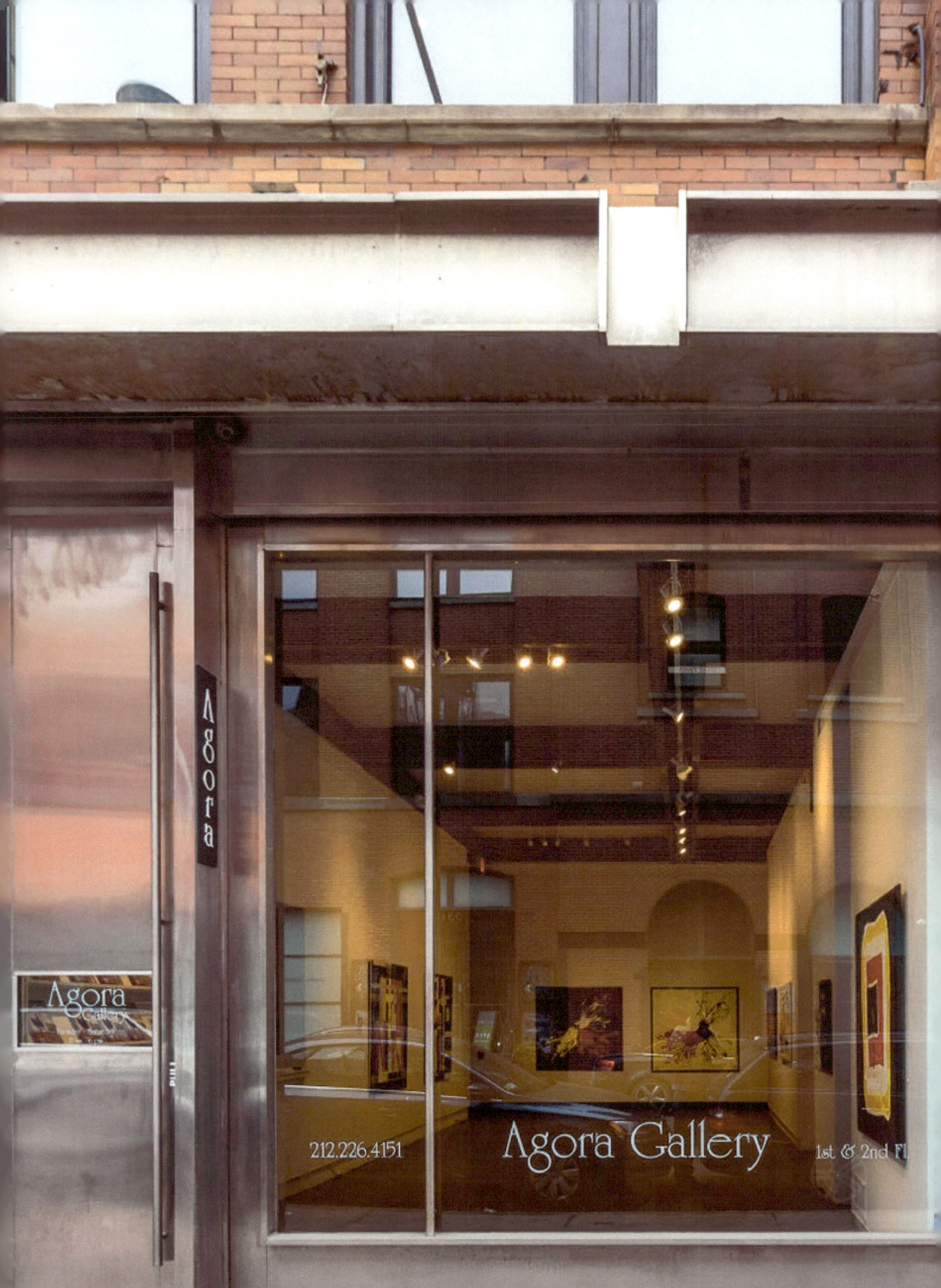
Agora
Agora Gallery
212.226.4151
Agora Gallery
1st & 2nd Fl

Stylistically placed between Matisse and Picasso, the oil paintings of Stephen Najda feature expressionistic figures representing the primitive self.

Every artist brings their unique perspectives into their works, and many times the greatest artists are the ones with multidisciplinary backgrounds. Stephen Najda brings to his artwork his own fascinating voice as a scientist. Holding multiple degrees in physics, Najda uses his research into quantum optics and photonics to imbue his unmistakable view beyond Cubist painting.

Segmenting forms into compelling color and bold line, Najda draws the viewer's focus into every individual element: both in those that make up the human form and those that make up a deeper sophisticated, developed composition. In this way, his works are highly intelligent explorations of form and representation, questioning what it means to be human and what it means for artwork to be transformative.

With oil on canvas and ink on paper, Najda's abstractions and improvisations on the human subject provoke an evocative dialog on the human condition. His subjects stand alone, in pairs, and small groupings. They interact with desolate and detached worlds, in an impenetrable landscape. A rare form smiles enigmatically, but the majority of Najda's characters wear thoughtful, sober faces, casting an ominous and disquieting hue over his deceptively colorful canvas. Through these figures, Najda examines the duality of the quantum world, exploring, he says, 'the boundary between imagination and consciences through the ambiguity of abstraction'.

Najda turned to painting, setting aside his naturally adventurous spirit in the mountains, after moving to the flat lands of Oxford, England. Najda found himself in a life drawing class and into a new world of art. He was able to quickly establish his unique style and voice, which has found him exhibiting across the UK and now in New York, showing a selection of his artwork at Agora Gallery in 2017.

- Angela Di Bello, Executive Director, Agora Gallery , Chelsea, New York

Agora Gallery

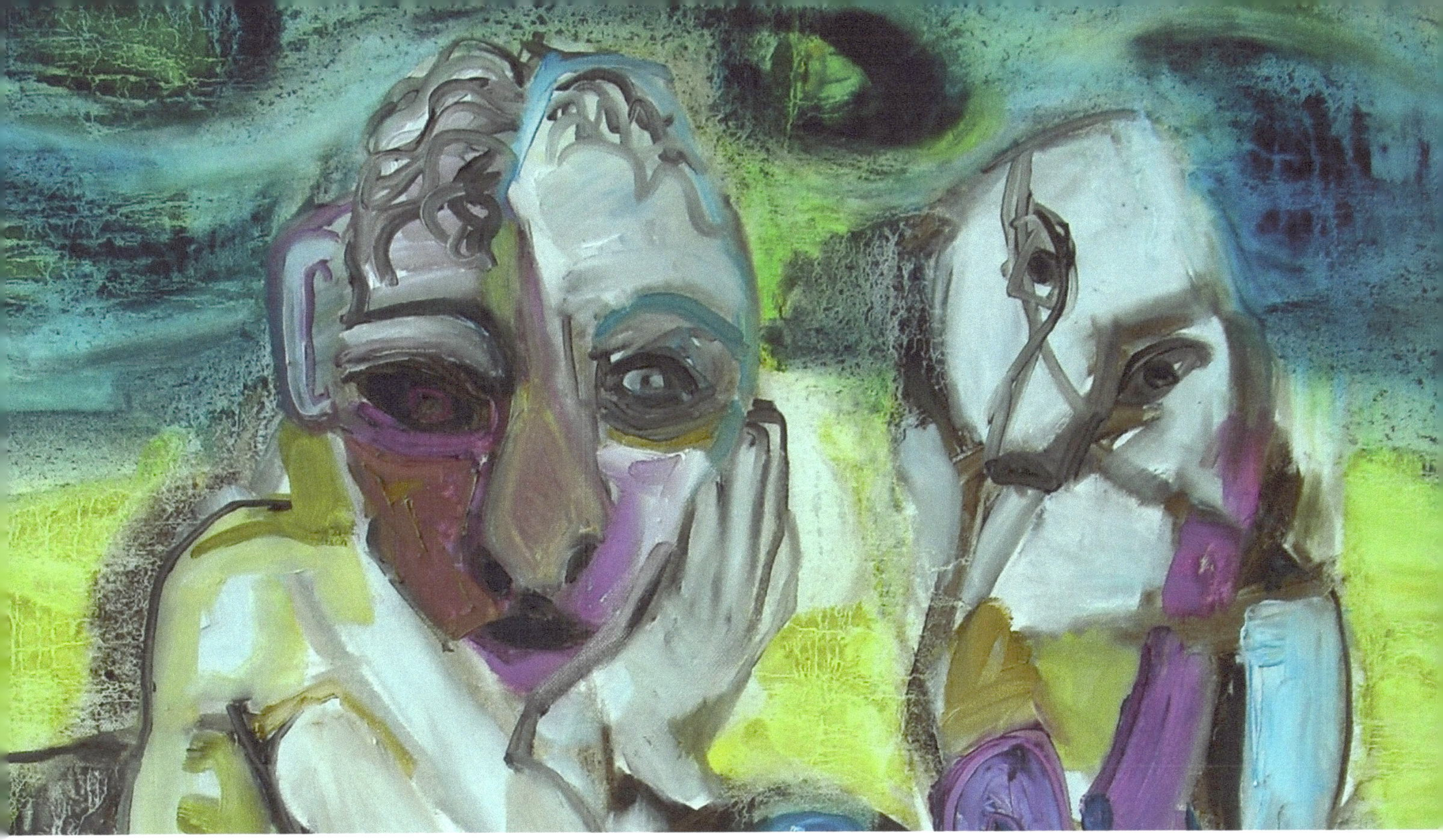

Unbound Perspectives
&
Persistence of Form

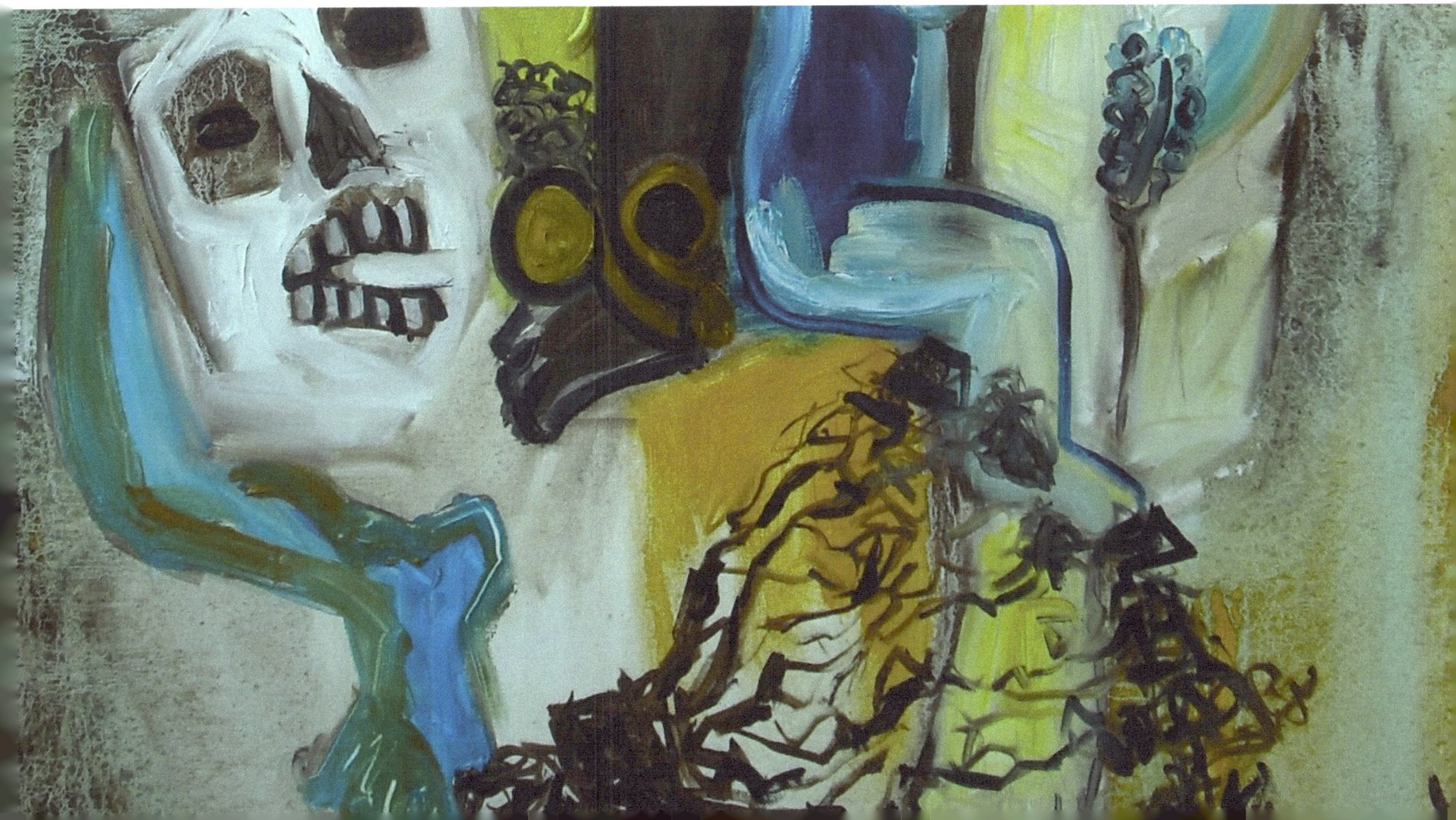

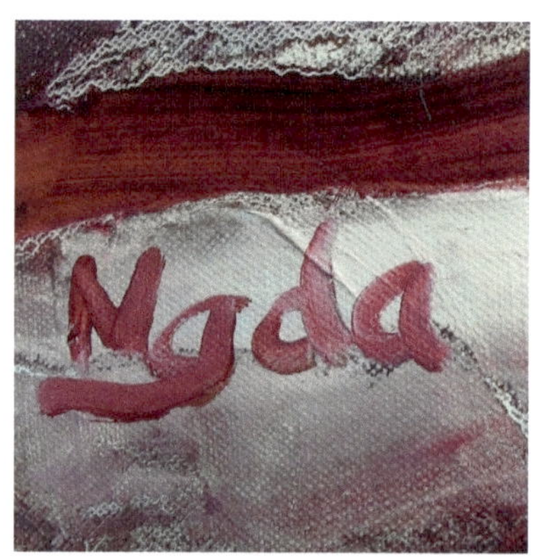

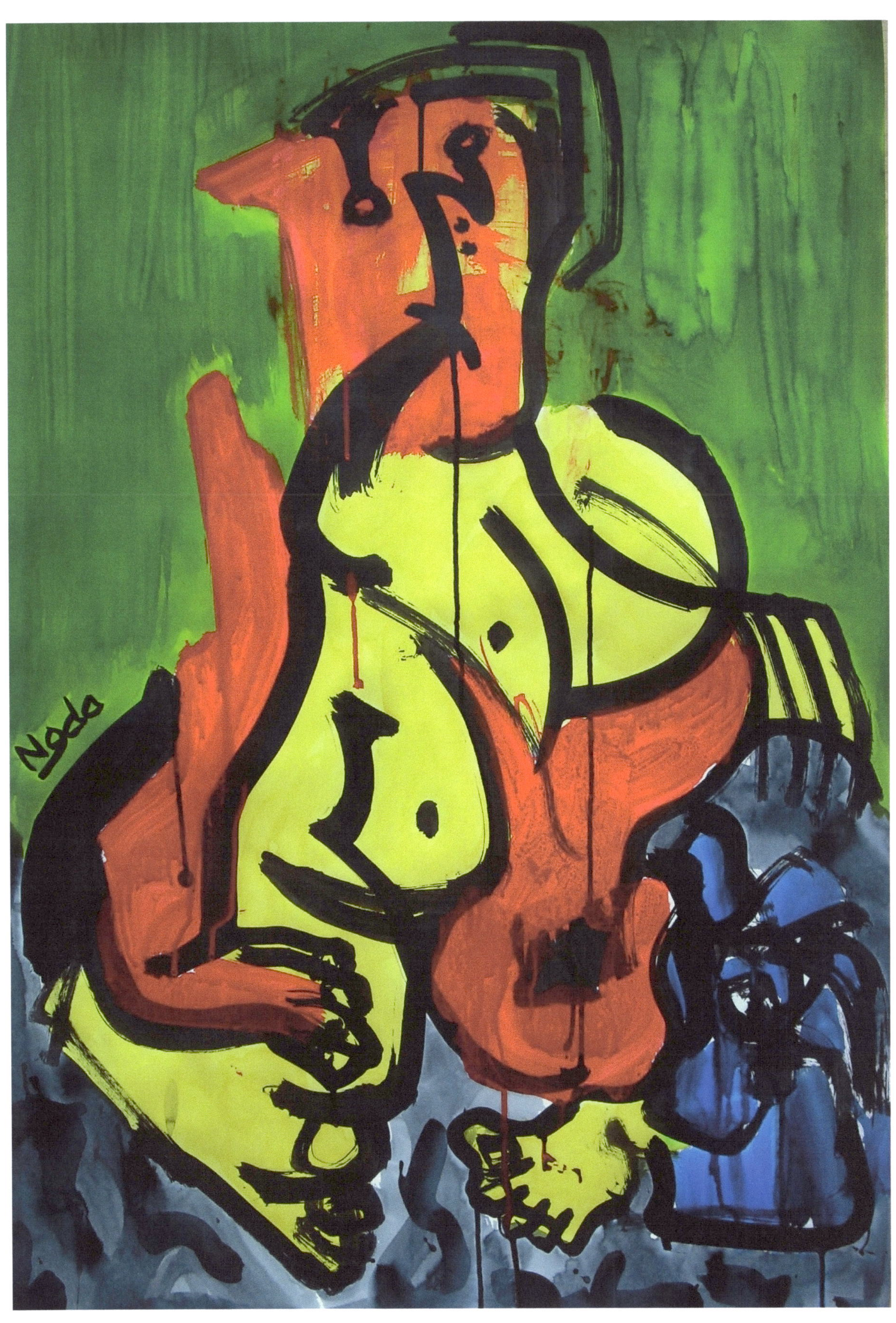

Technique: Ink on paper - Size: 60 cm x 80 cm - Year: 2014

Detail 1

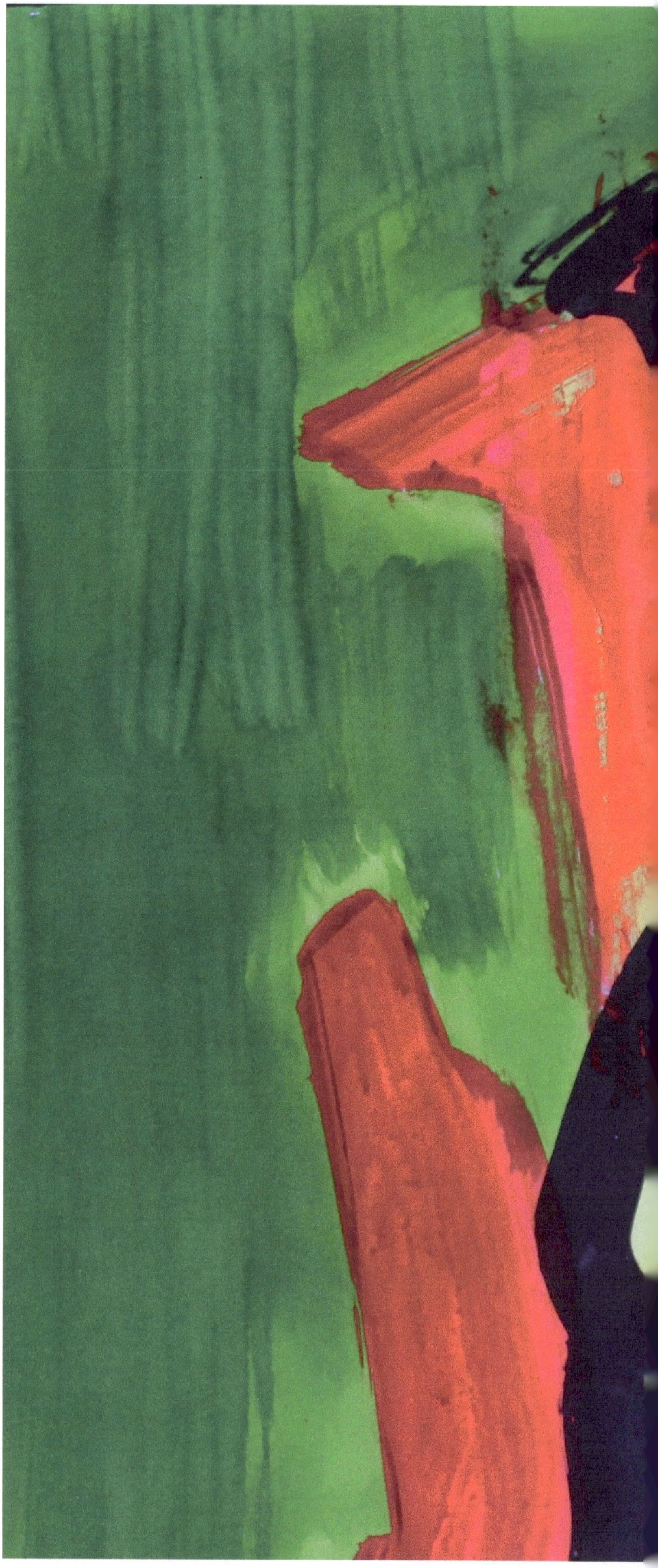

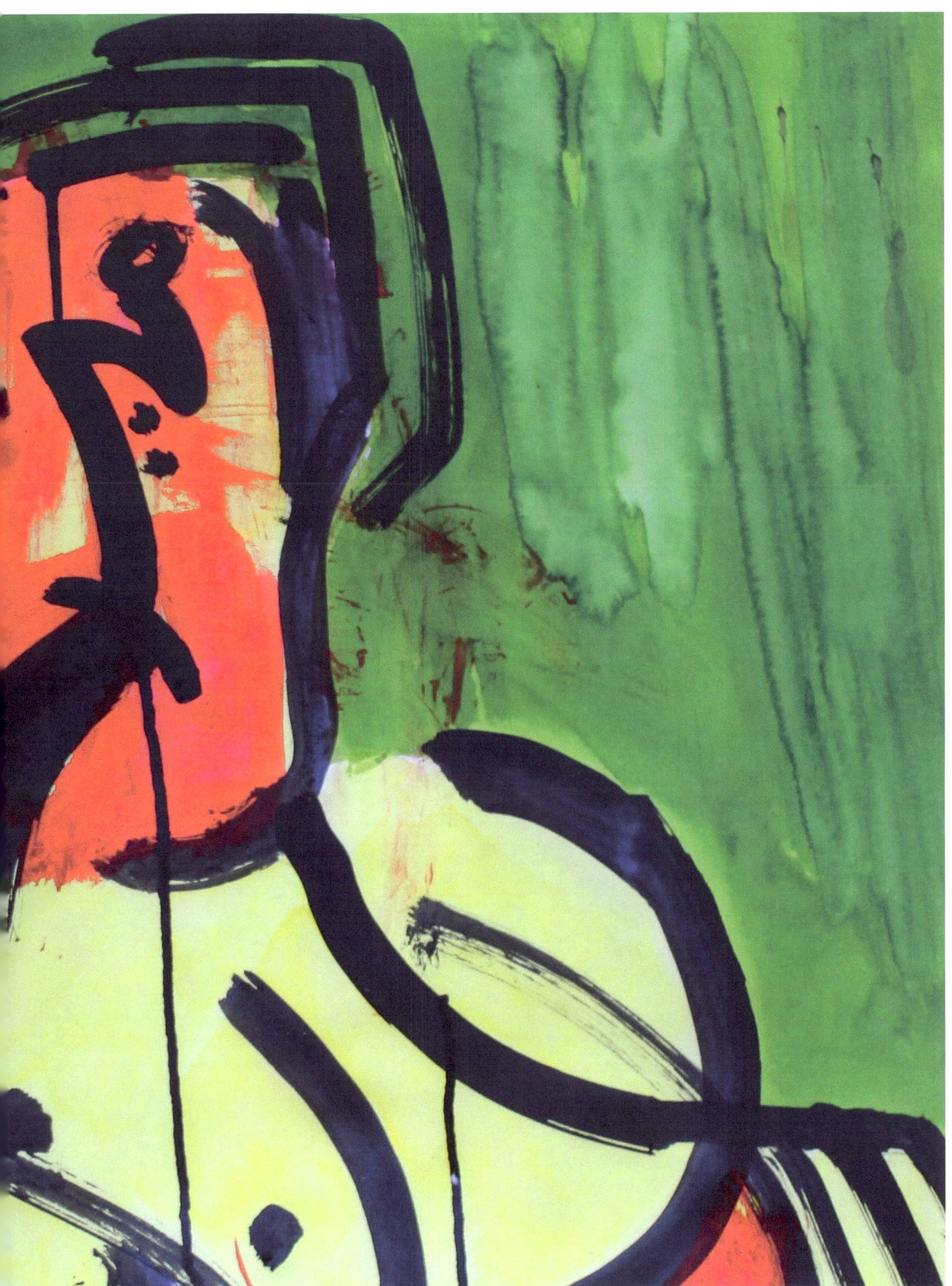

Detail 2

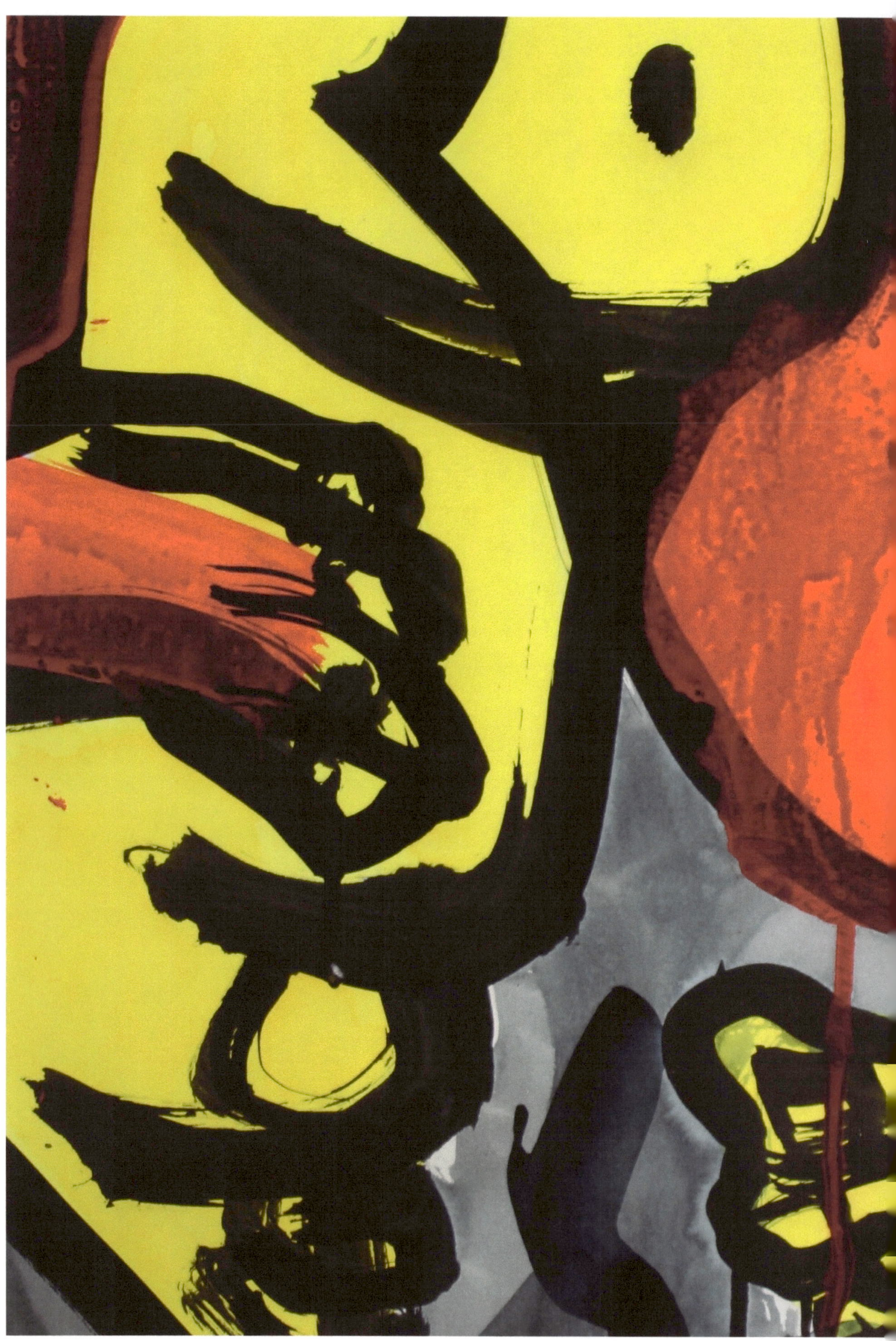

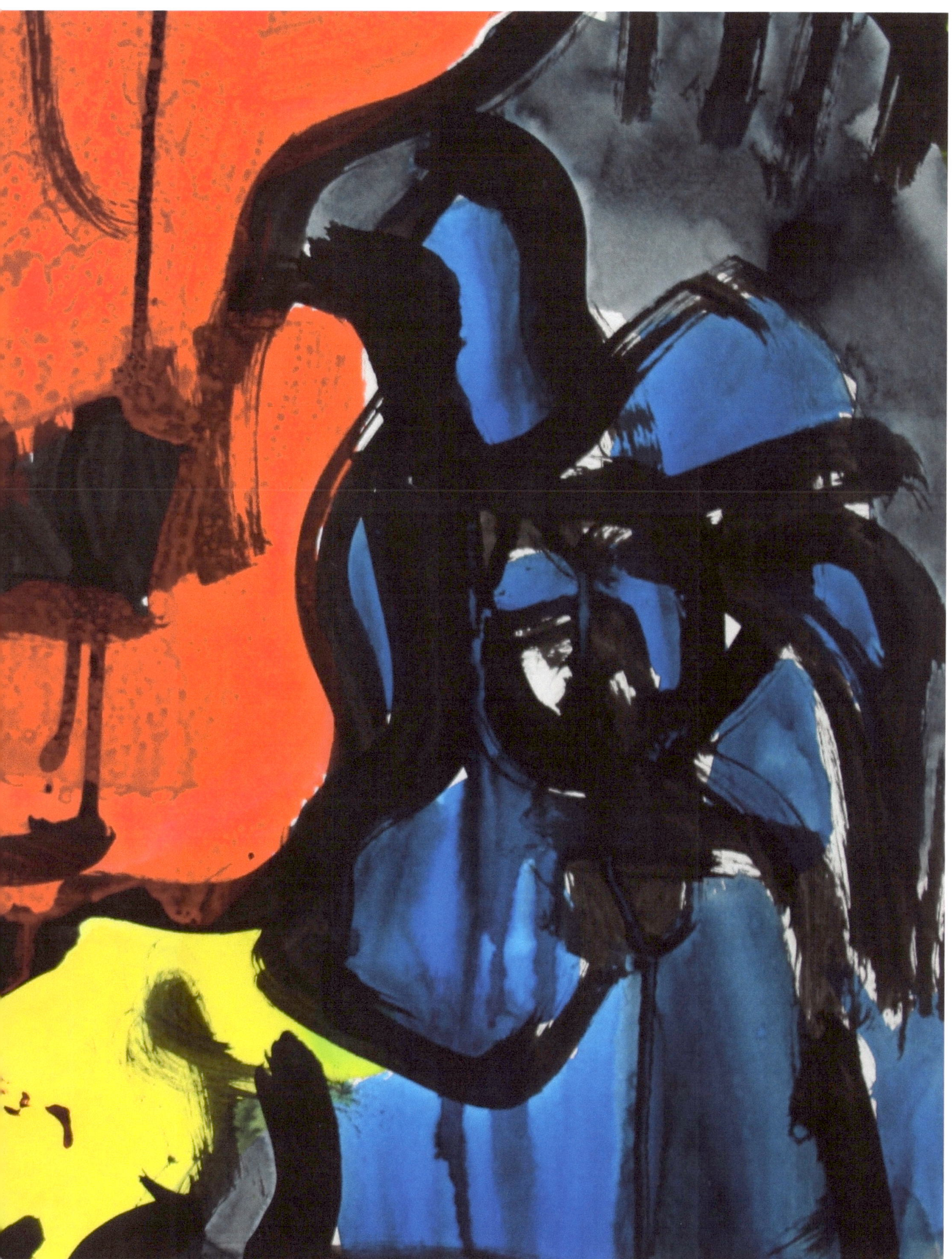

Detail 3

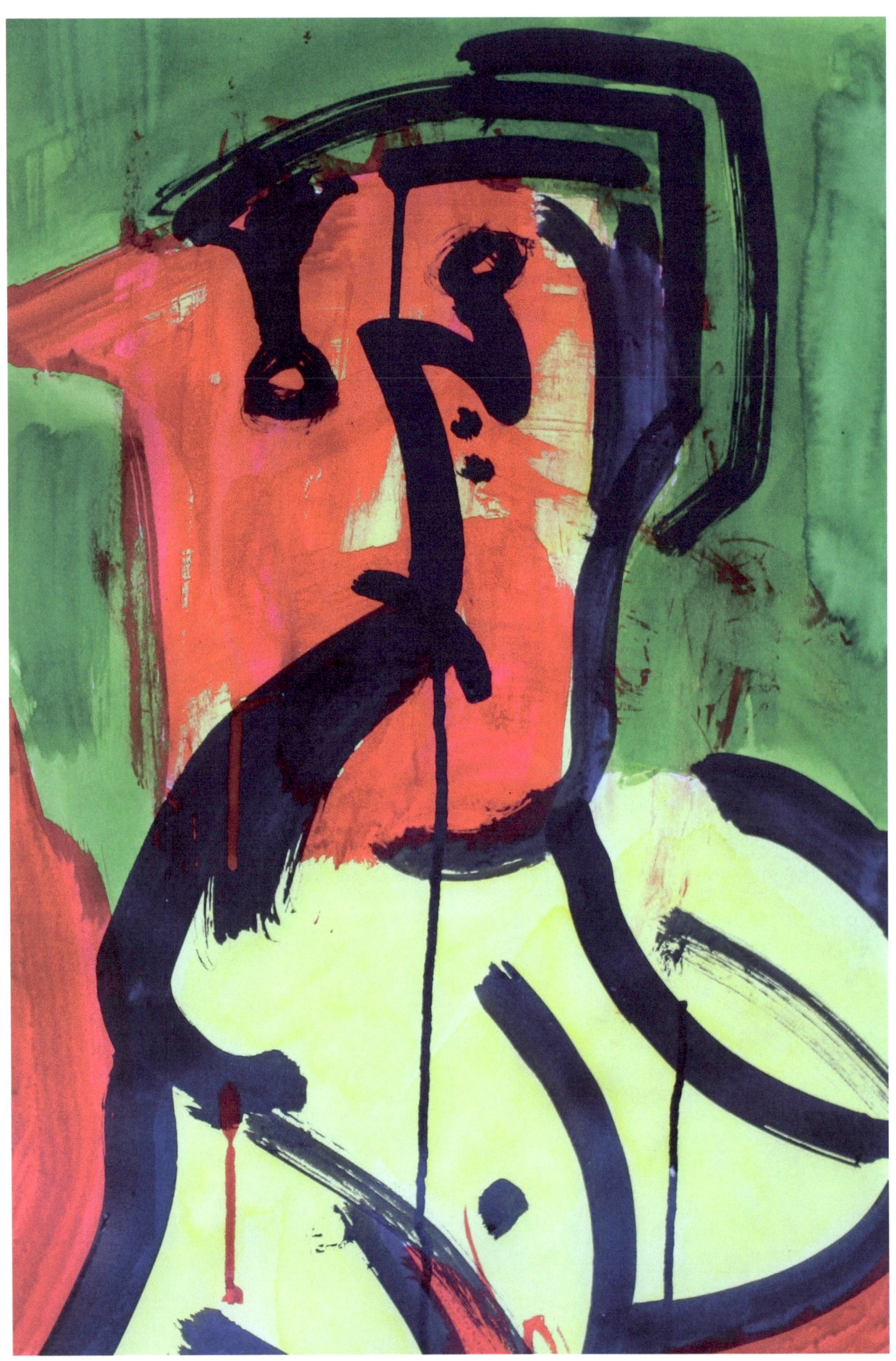

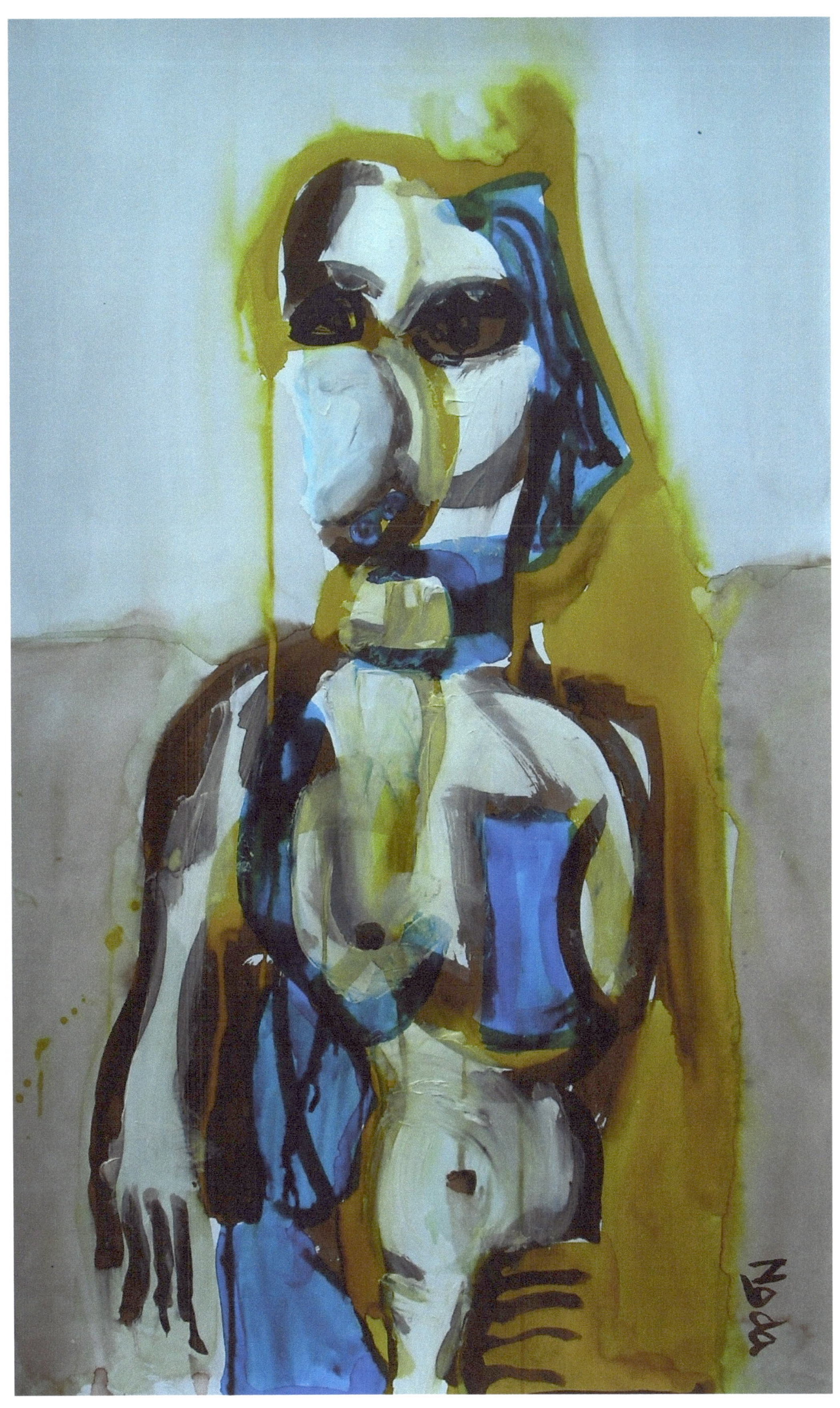

Technique: Ink on paper - Size: 60 cm x 80 cm - Year: 2014

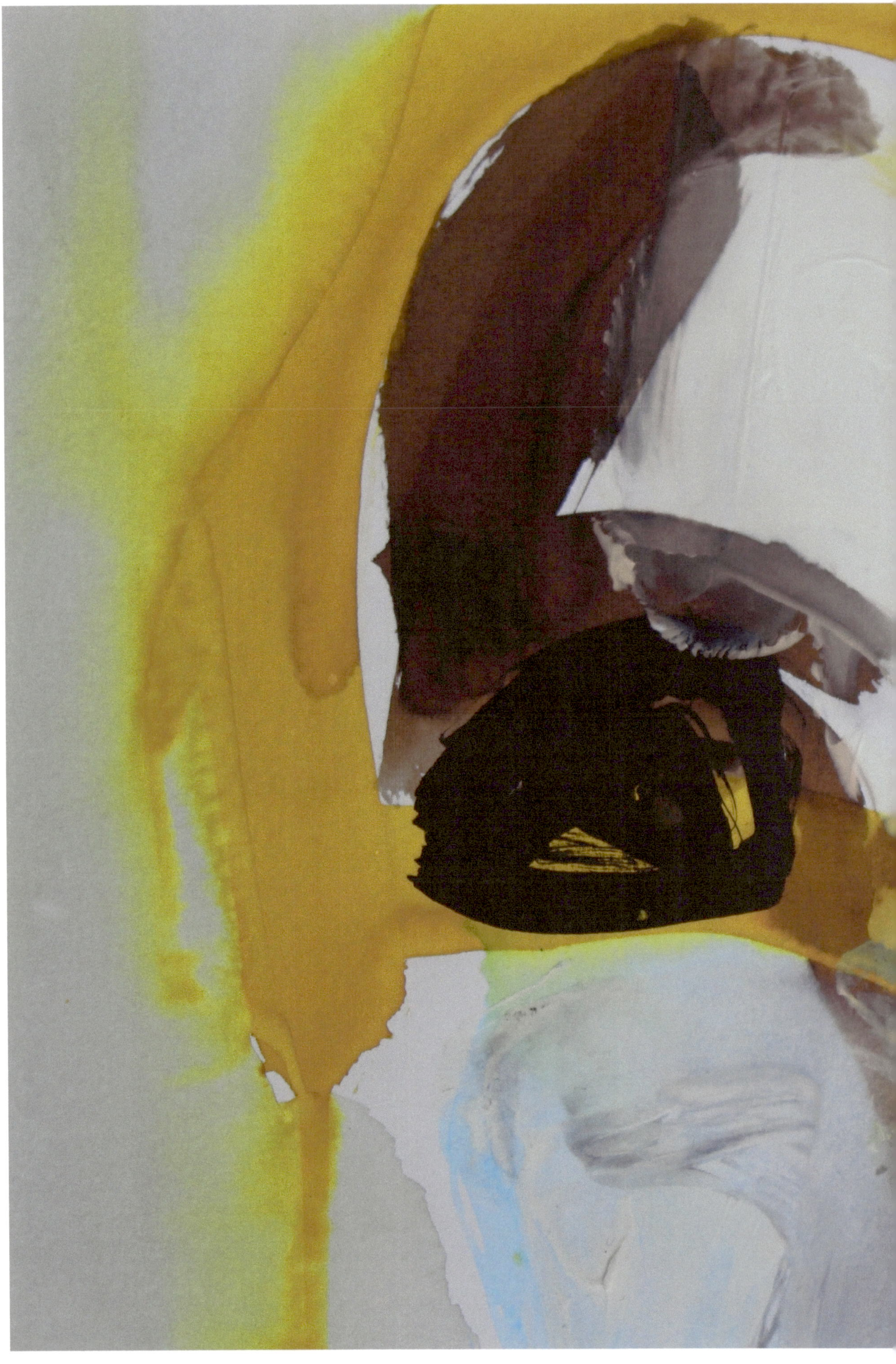

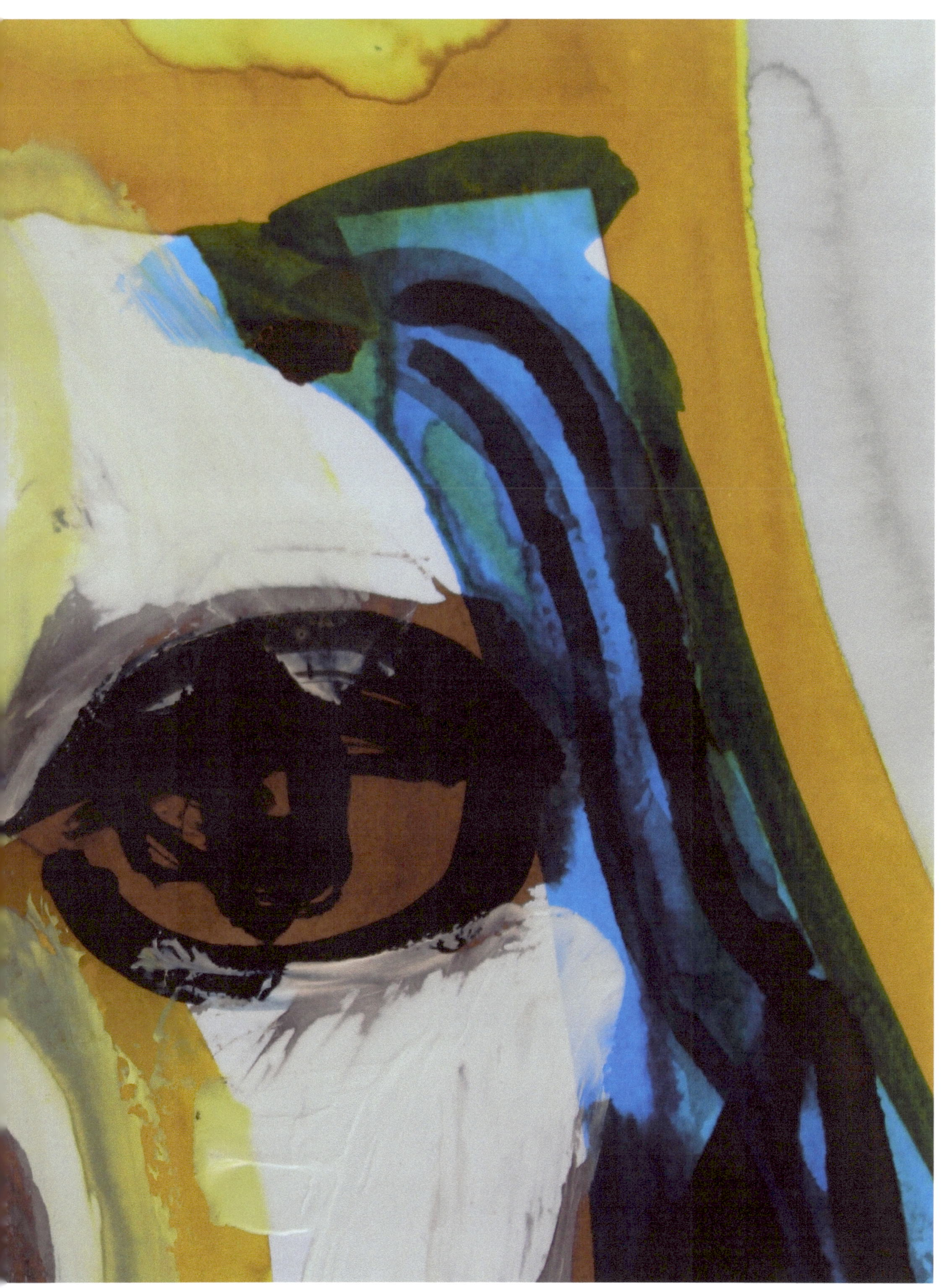

Detail 2

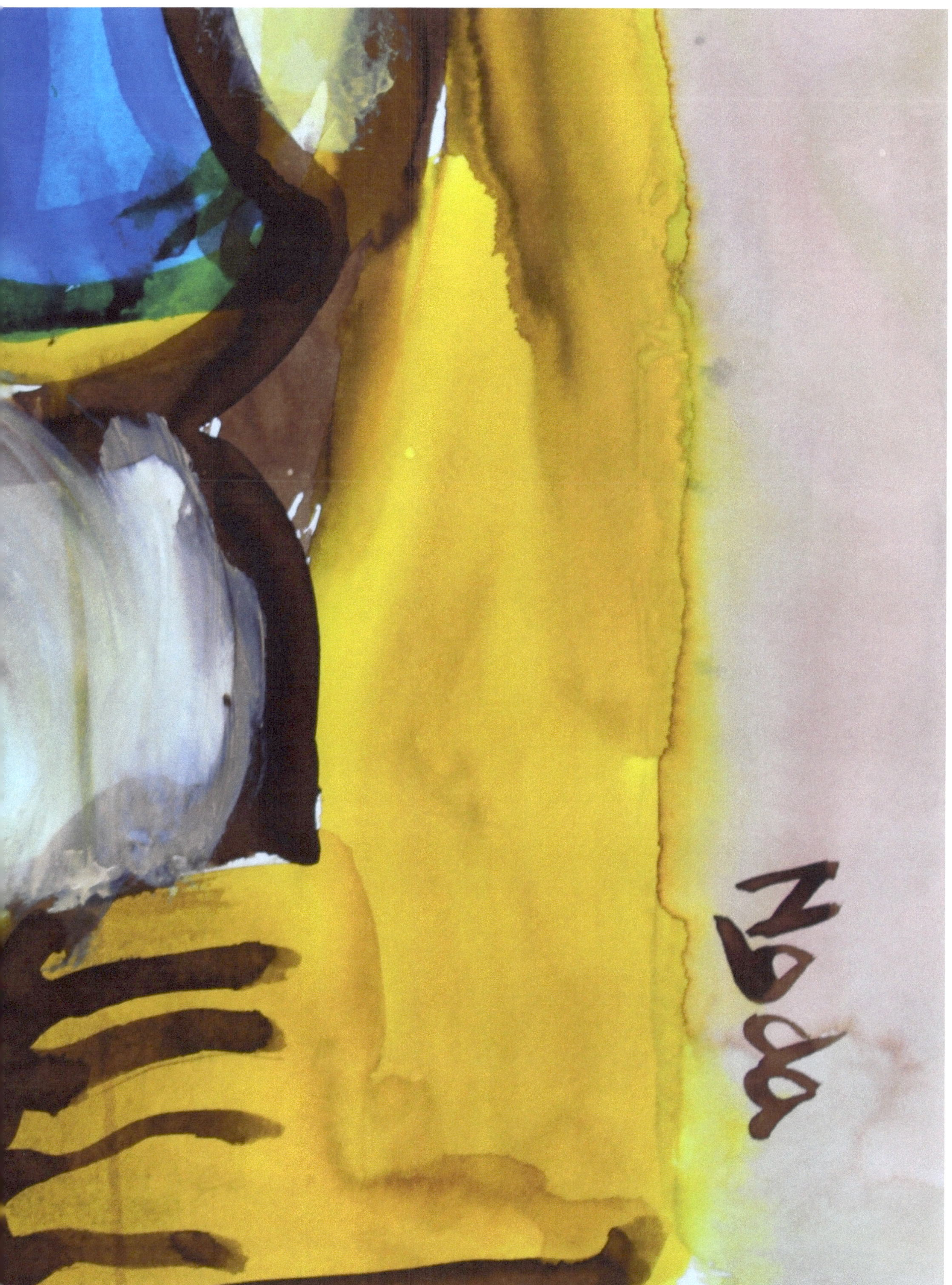

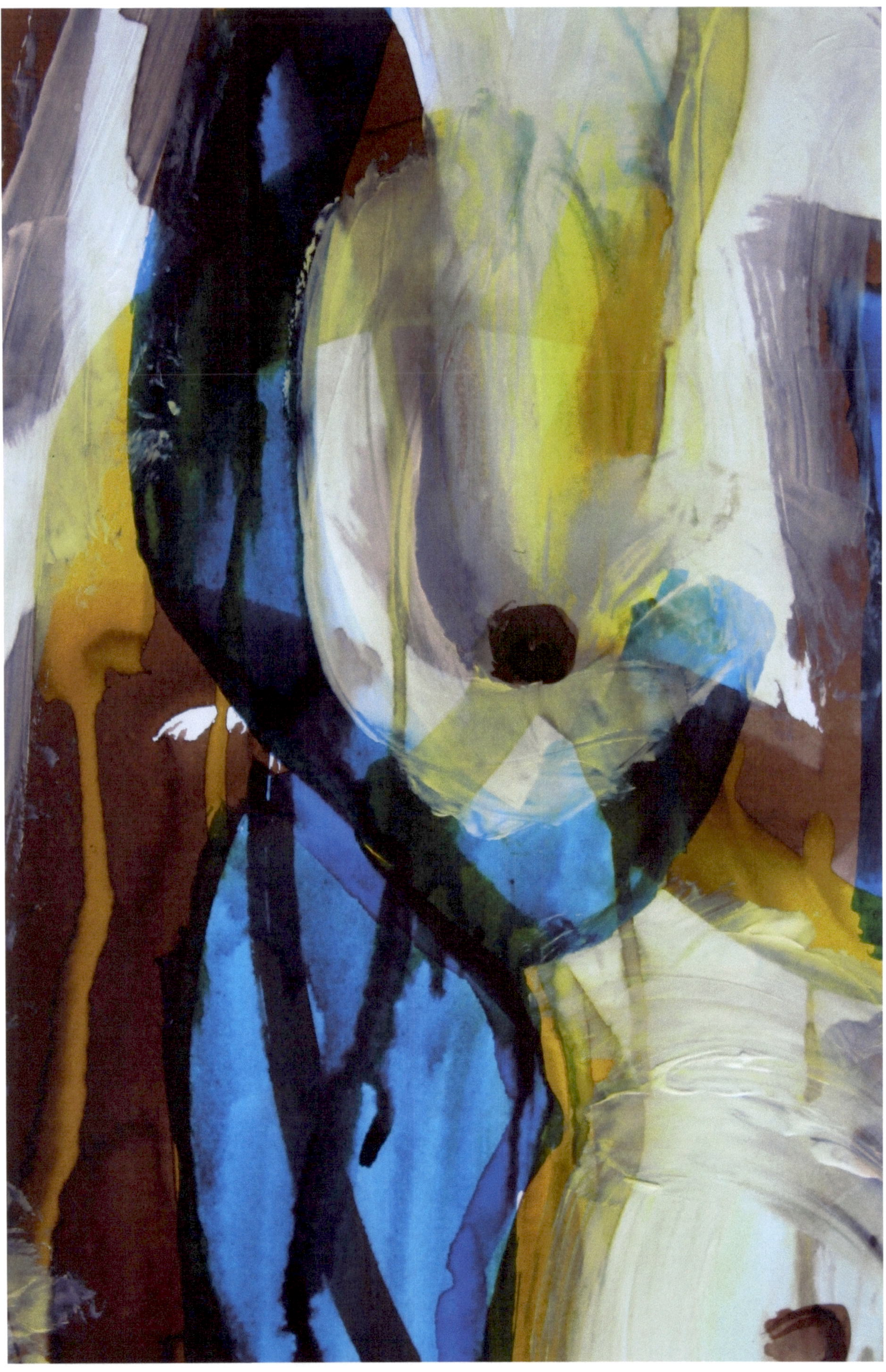

Detail 3

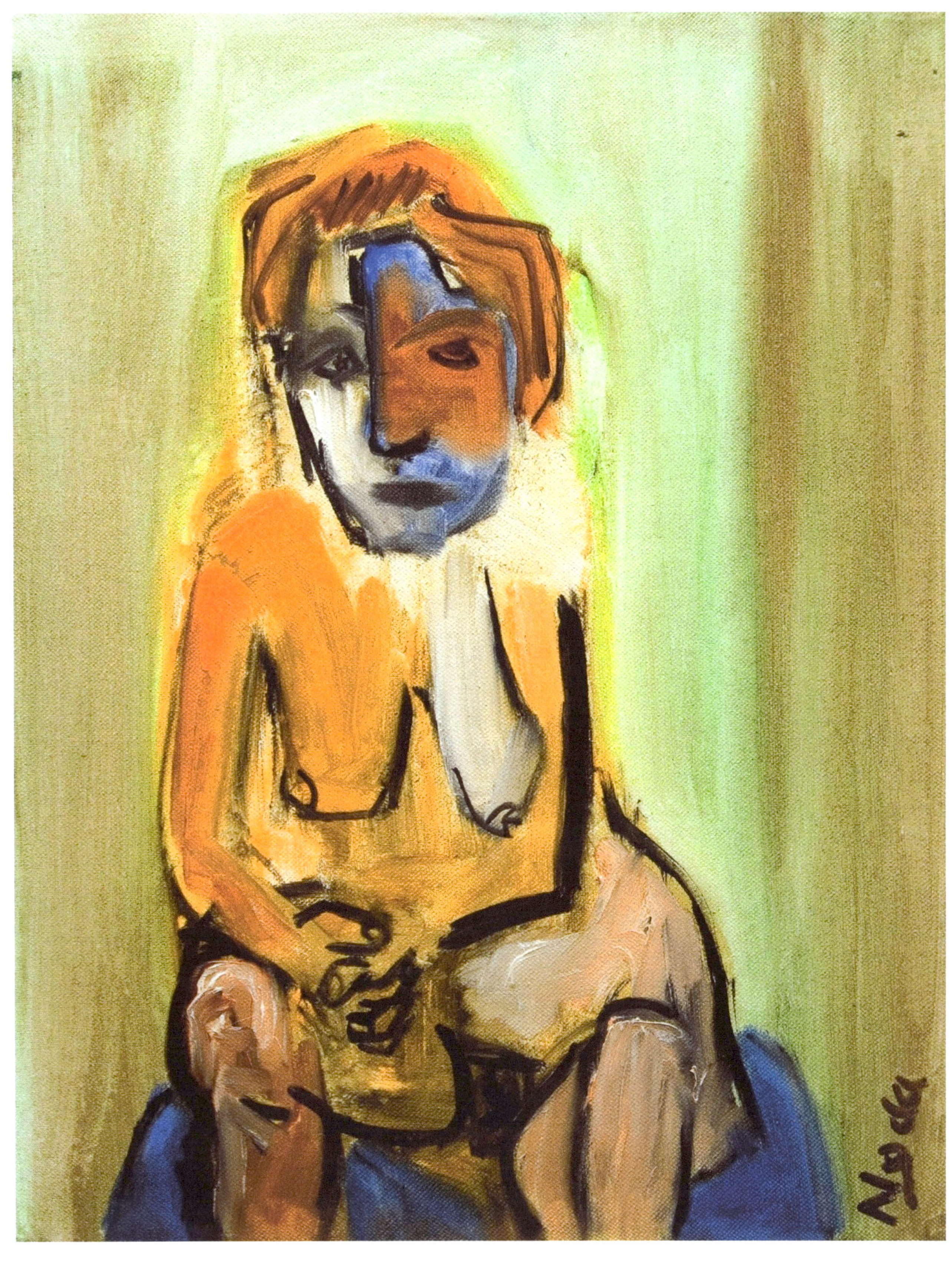

Technique: Oil painting on canvas
Size: 40 cm x 40 cm
Year: 2014

Detail 1

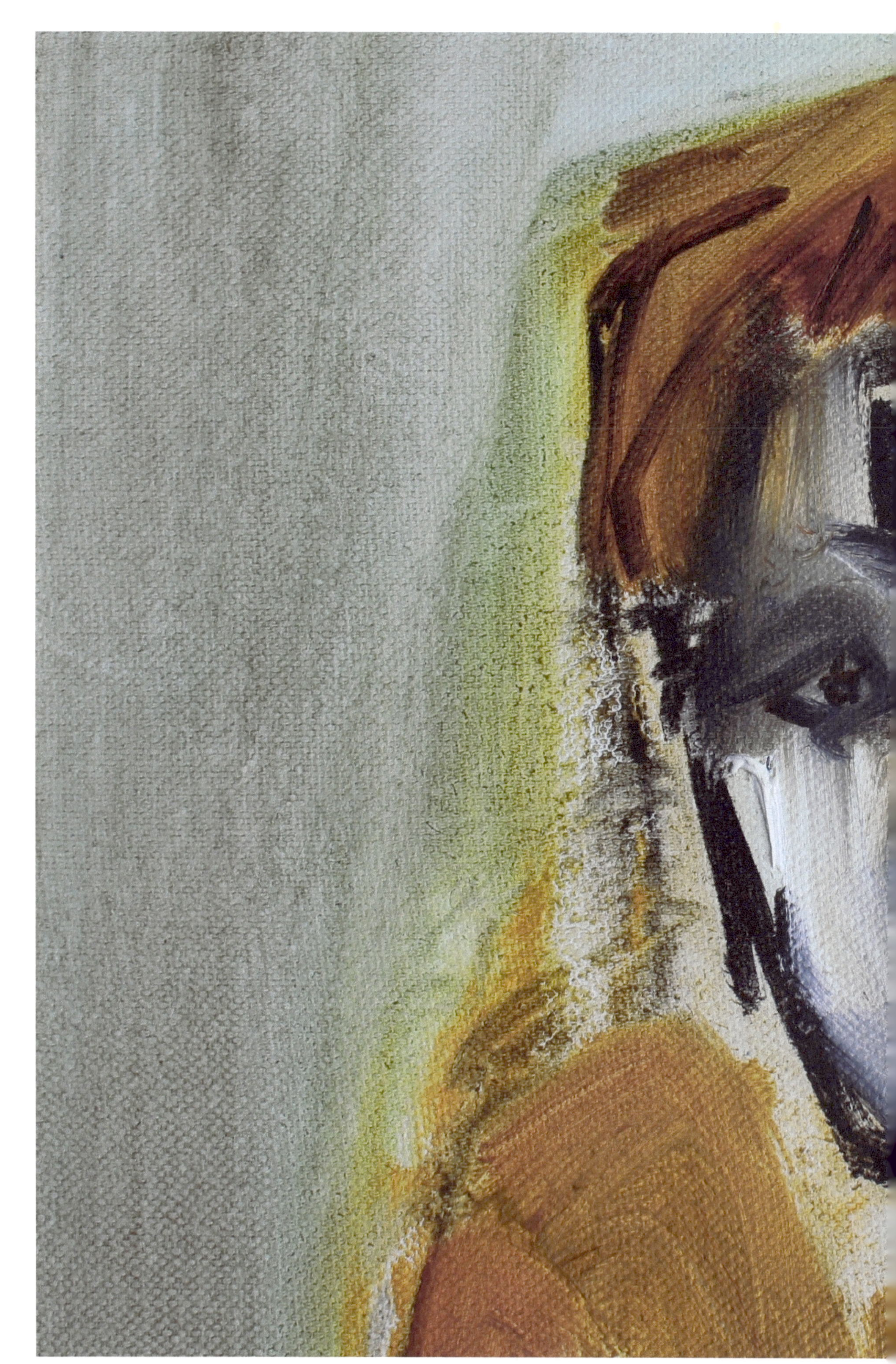

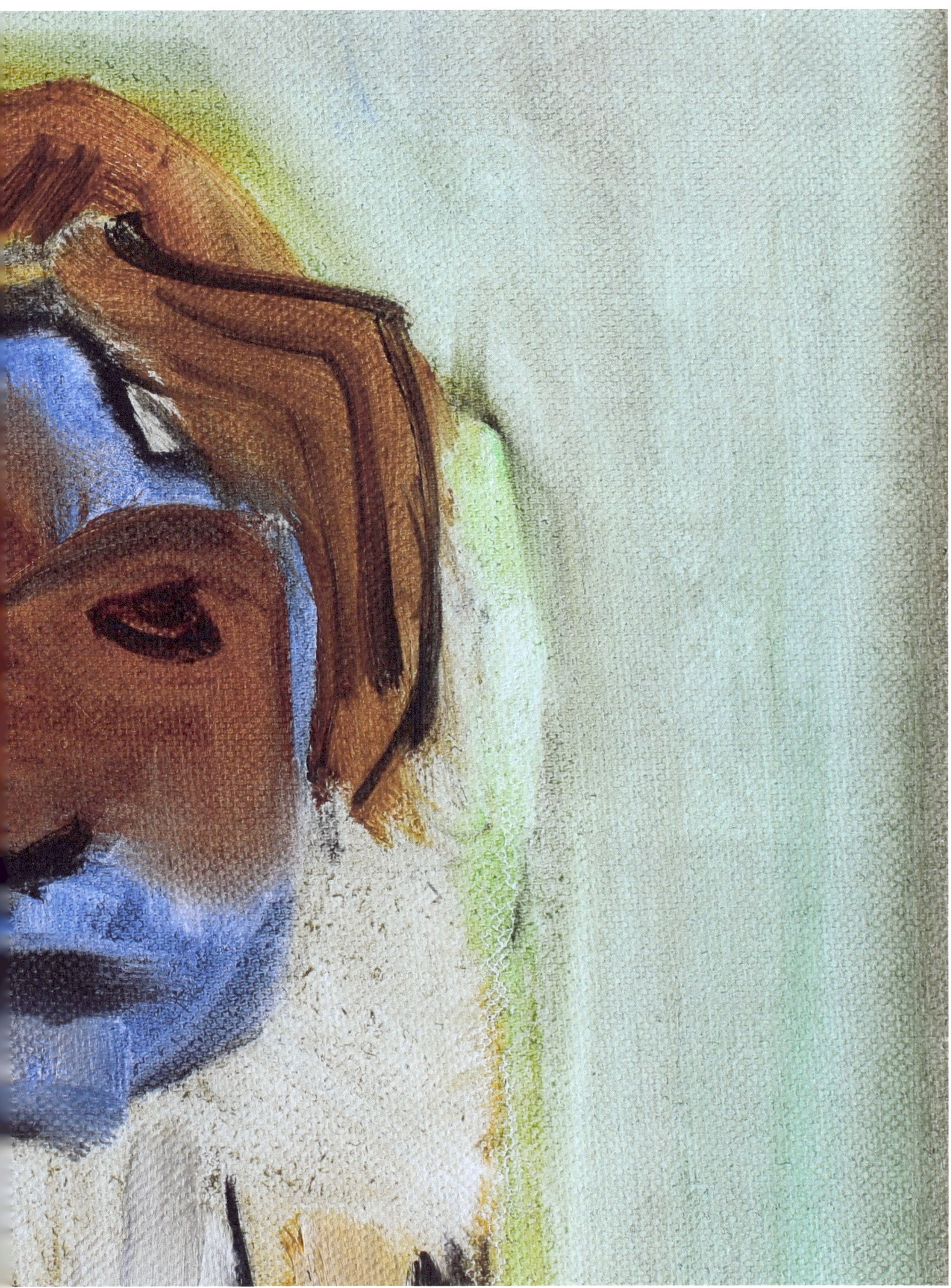

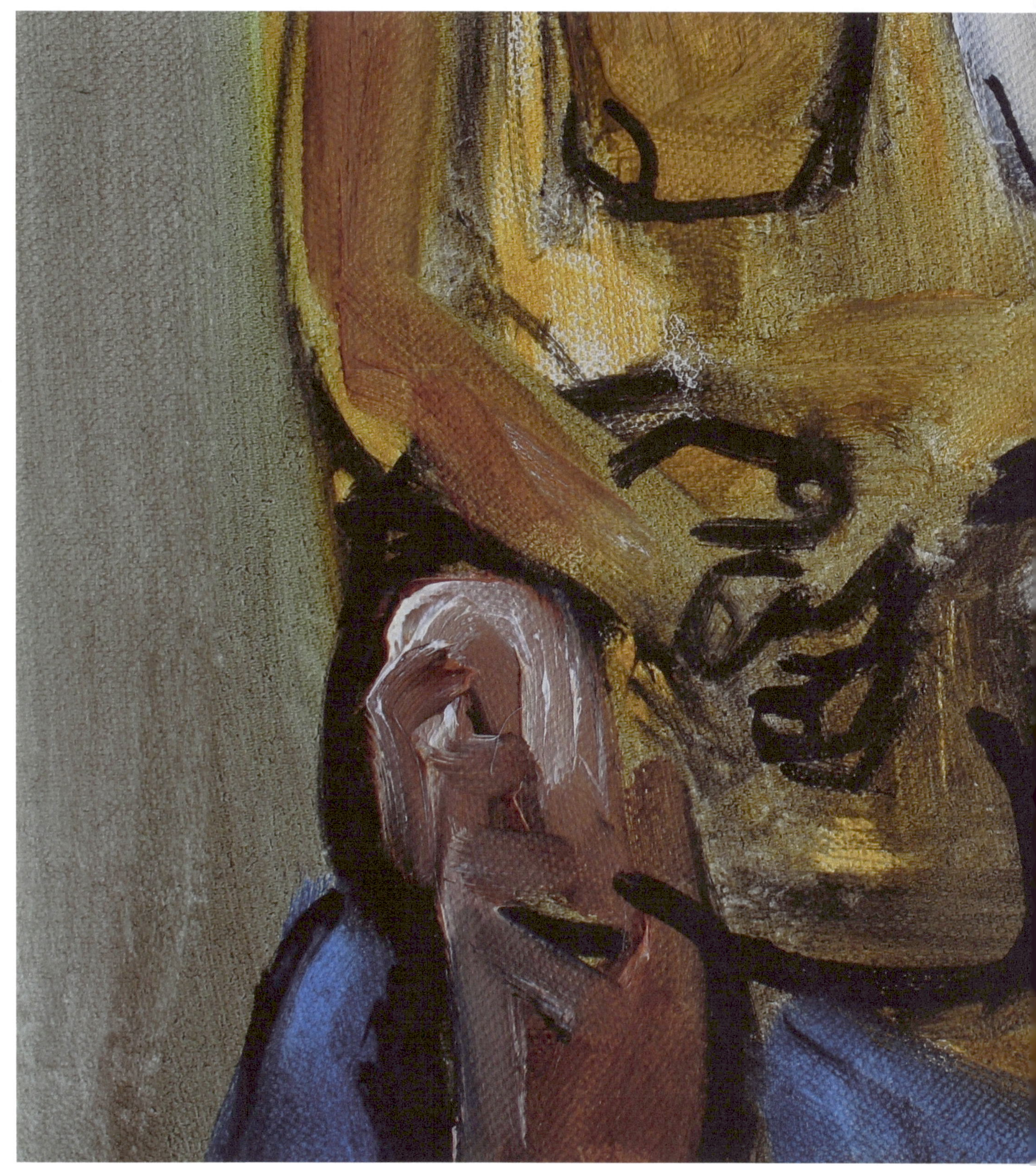

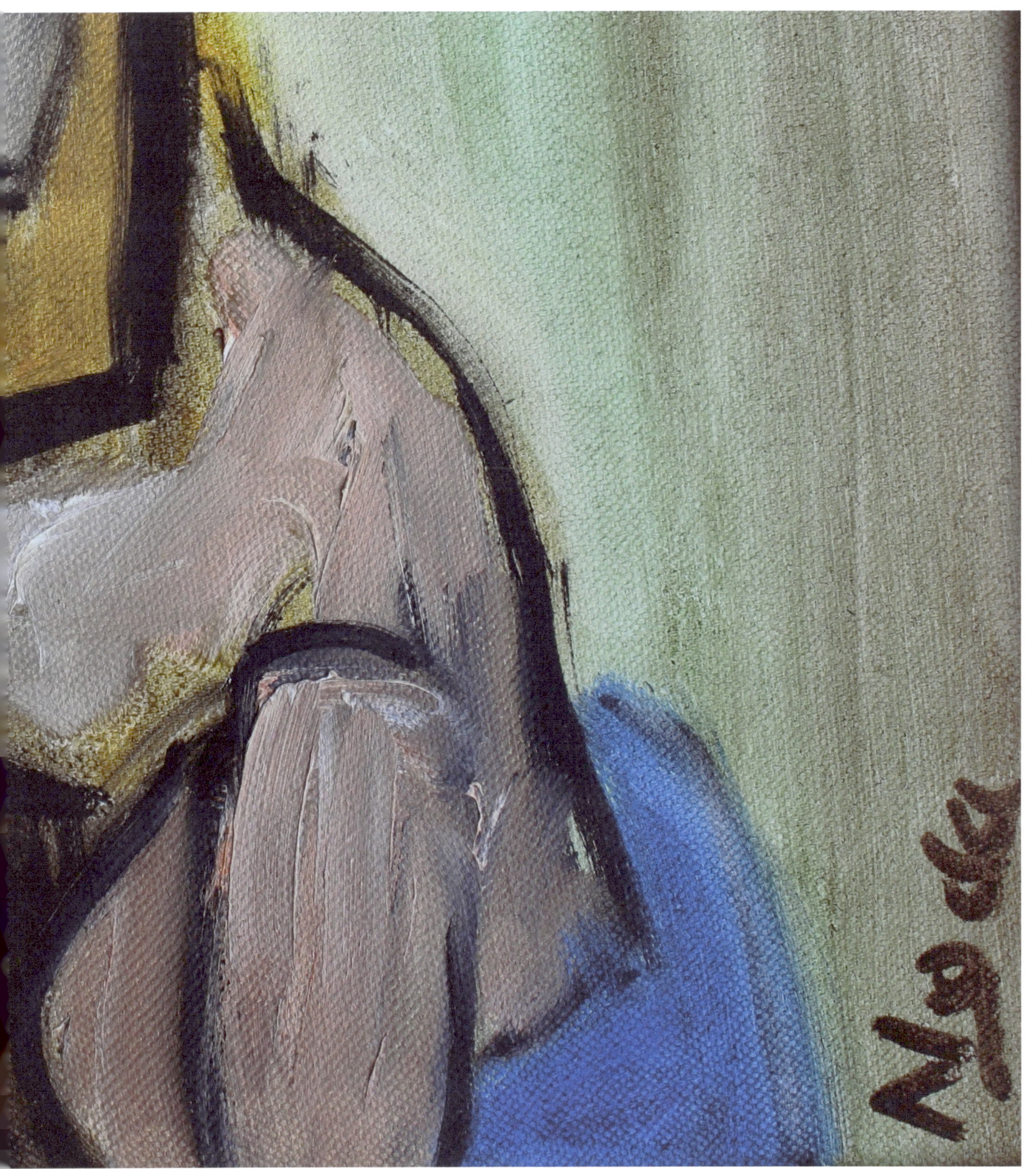

Detail 3

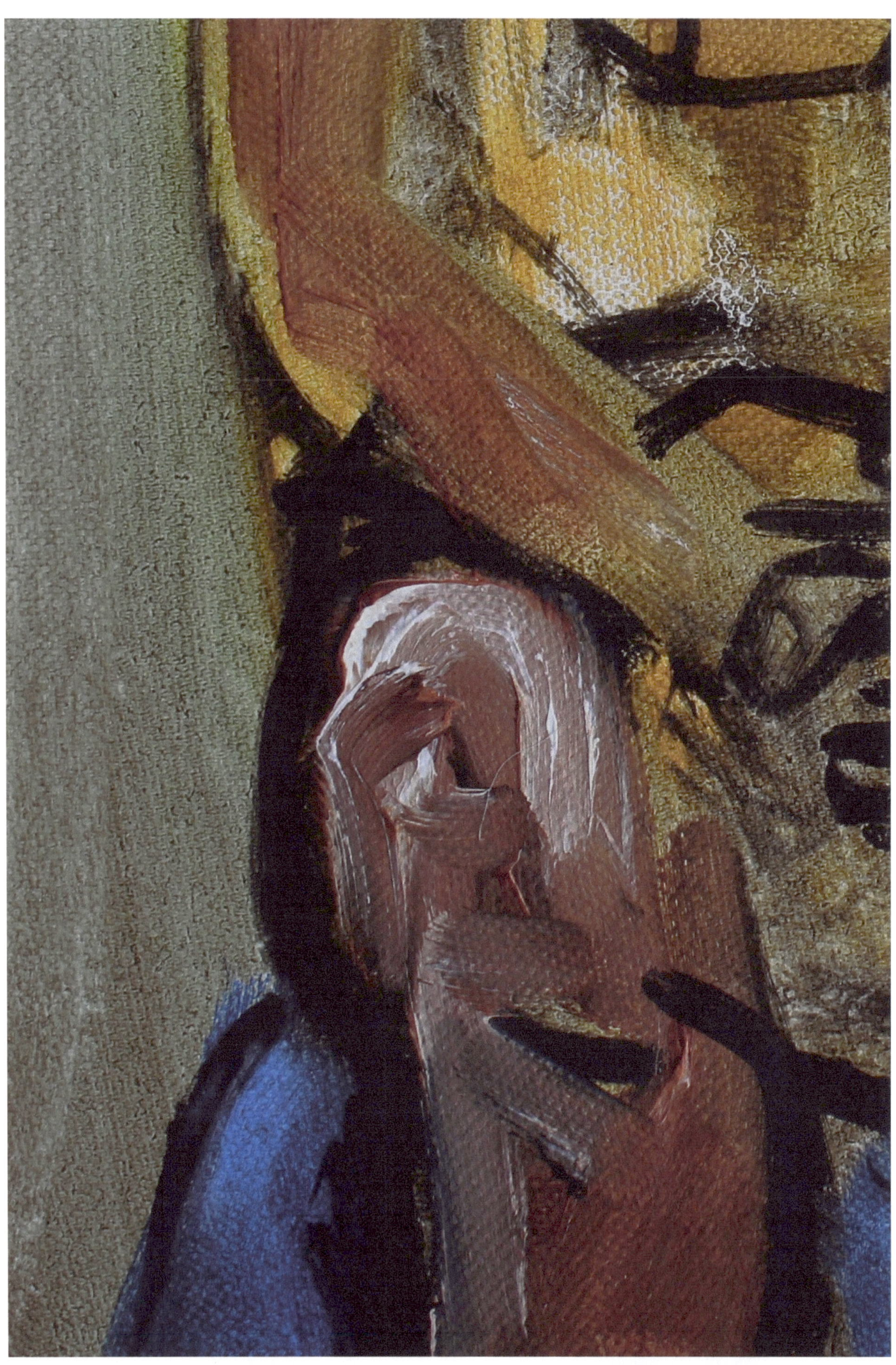

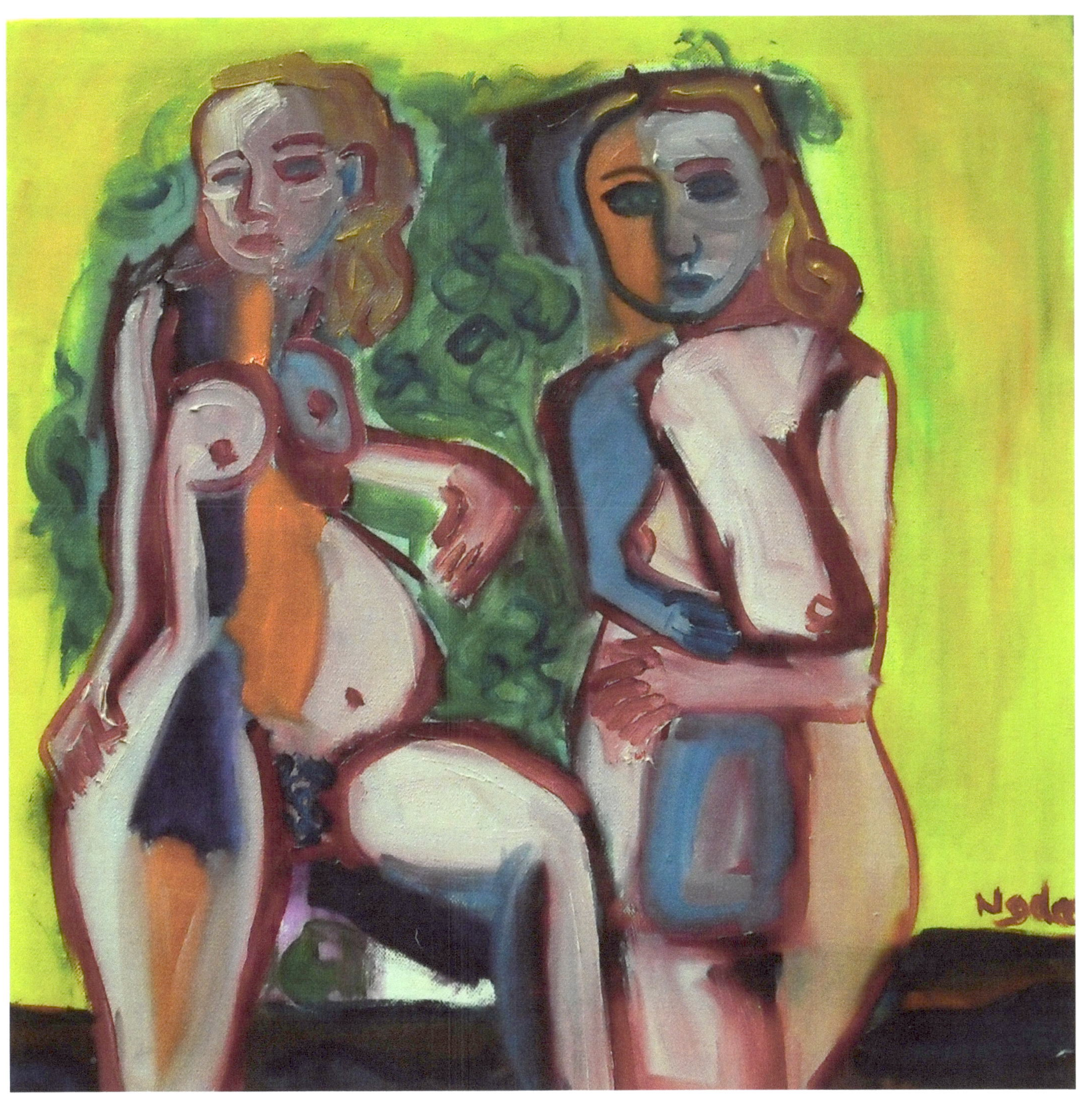

Technique: Oil painting on canvas
Size: 40 cm x 40 cm
Year: 2014

Detail 1

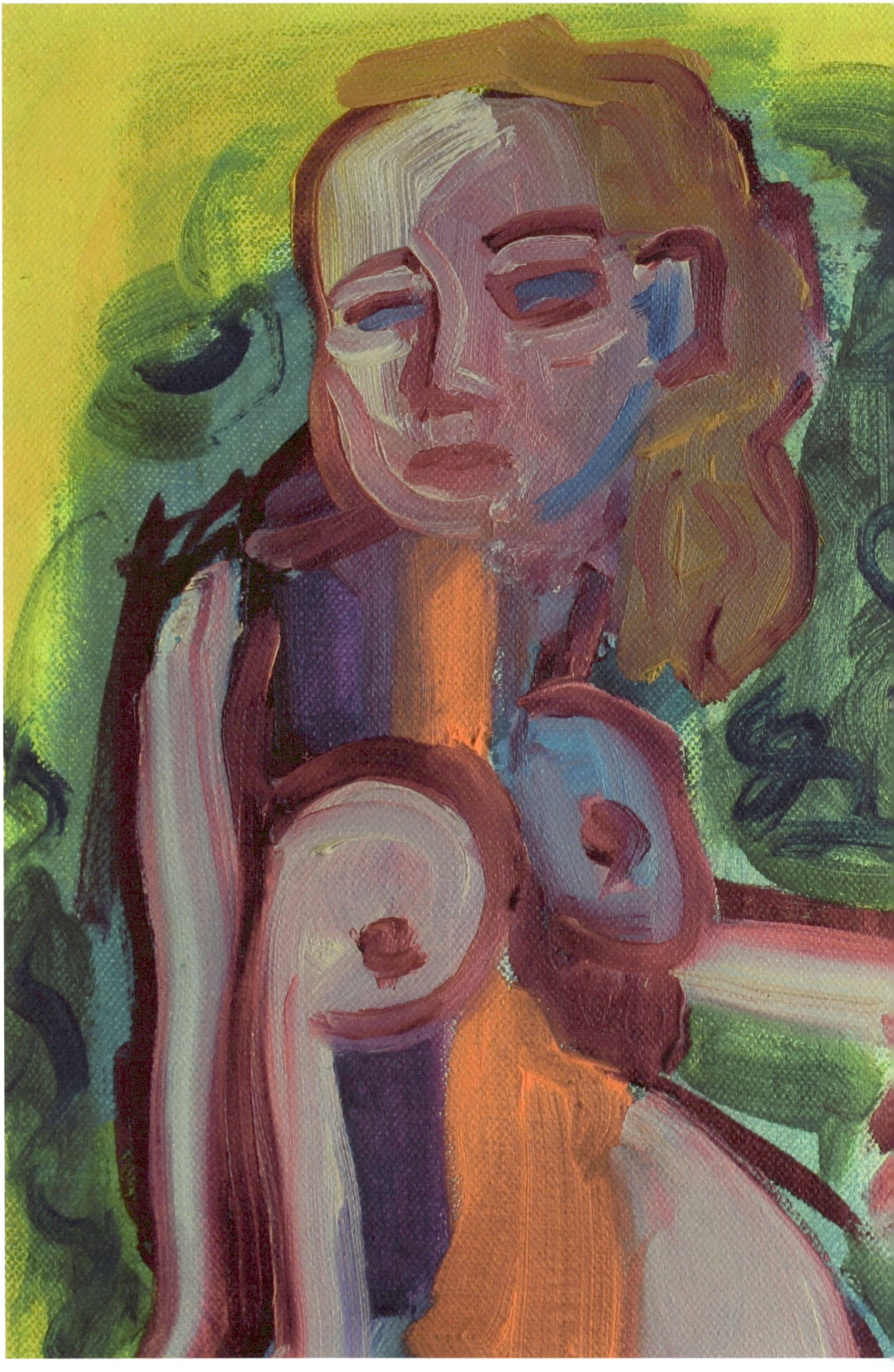

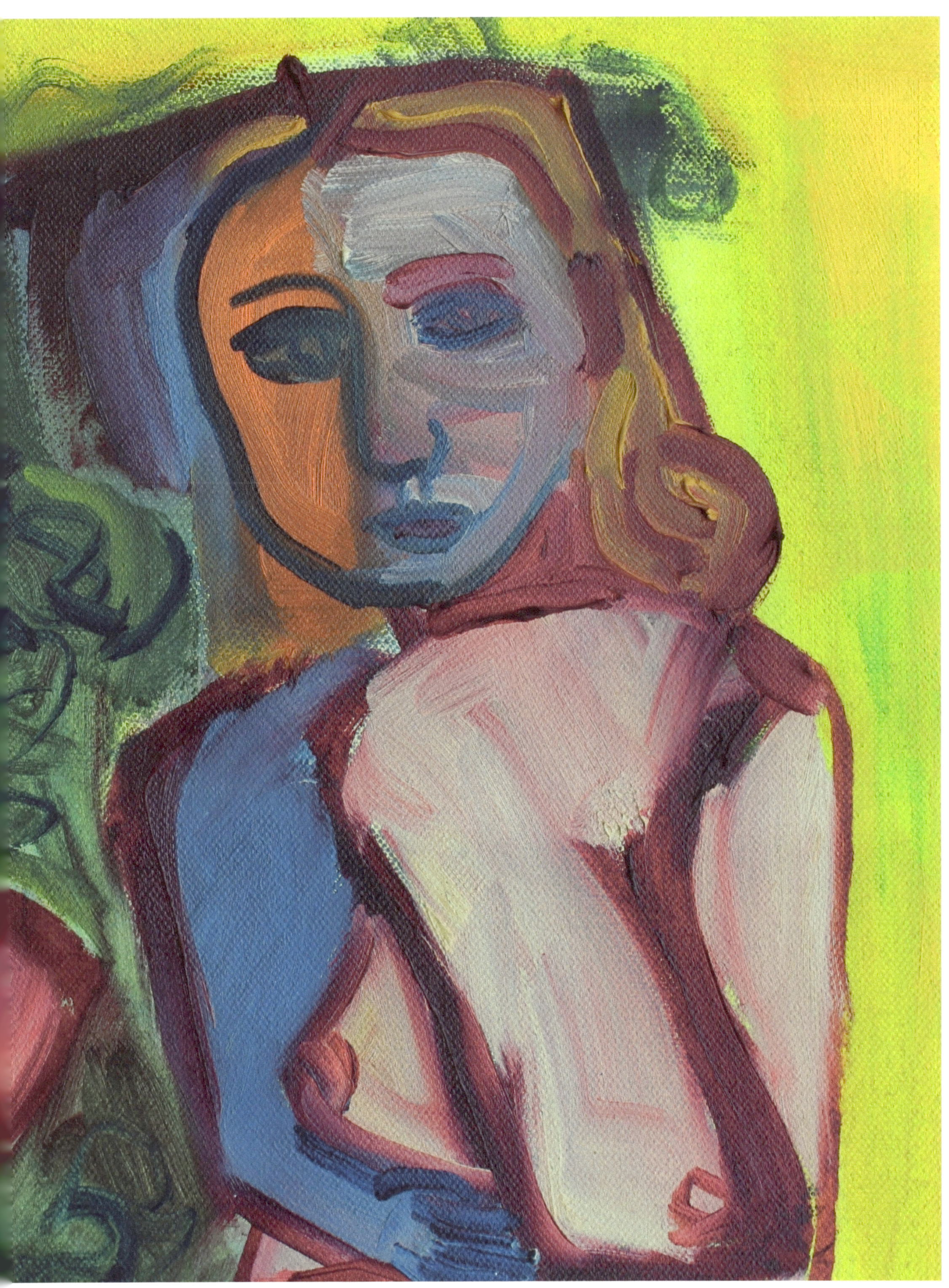

Detail 2

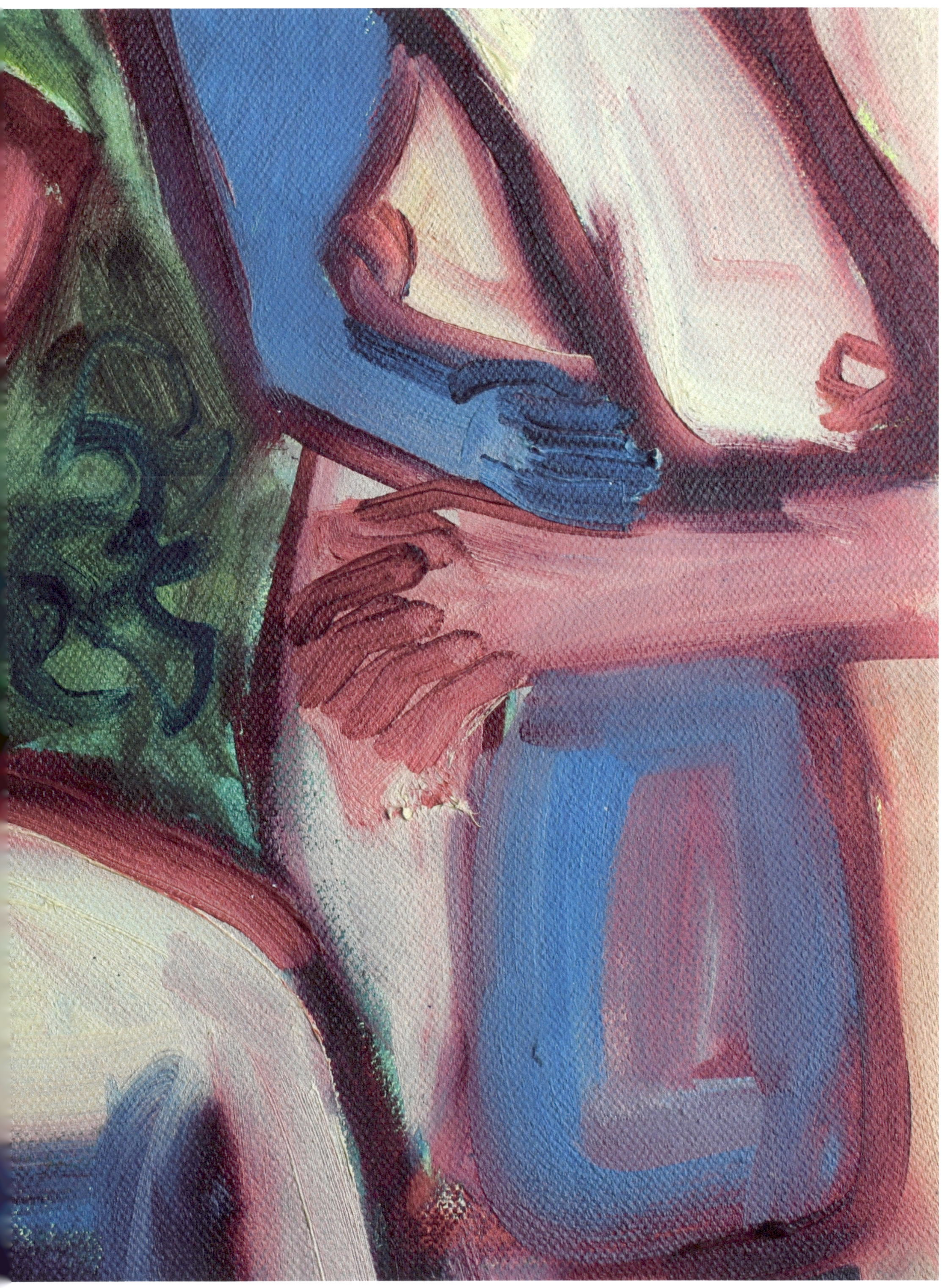

Detail 3

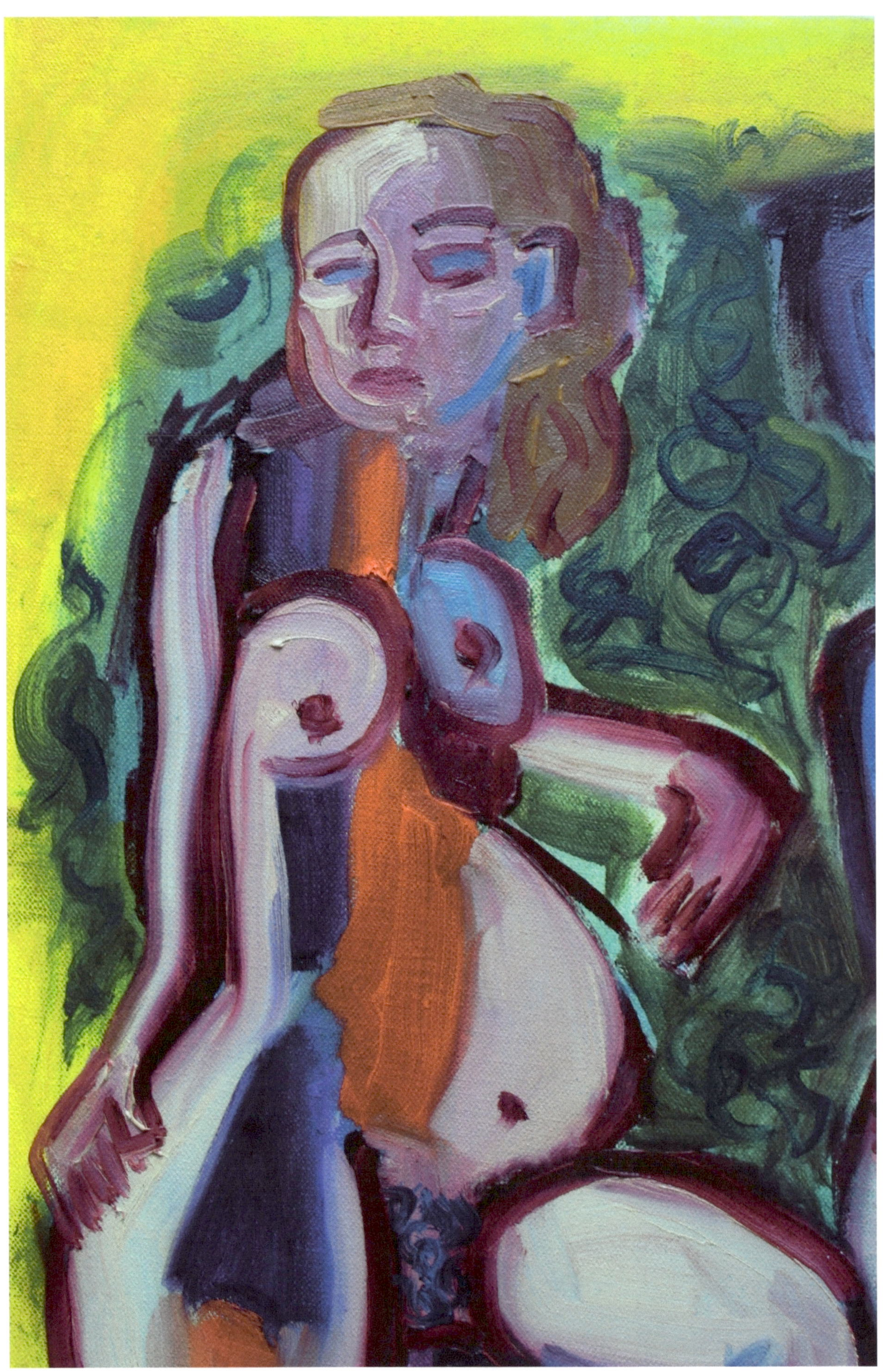

"MAN WITH SKULL, WOMAN WITH CHILD
AND THE TUMBLE WEED OF LIFE IN THE MIDDLE"

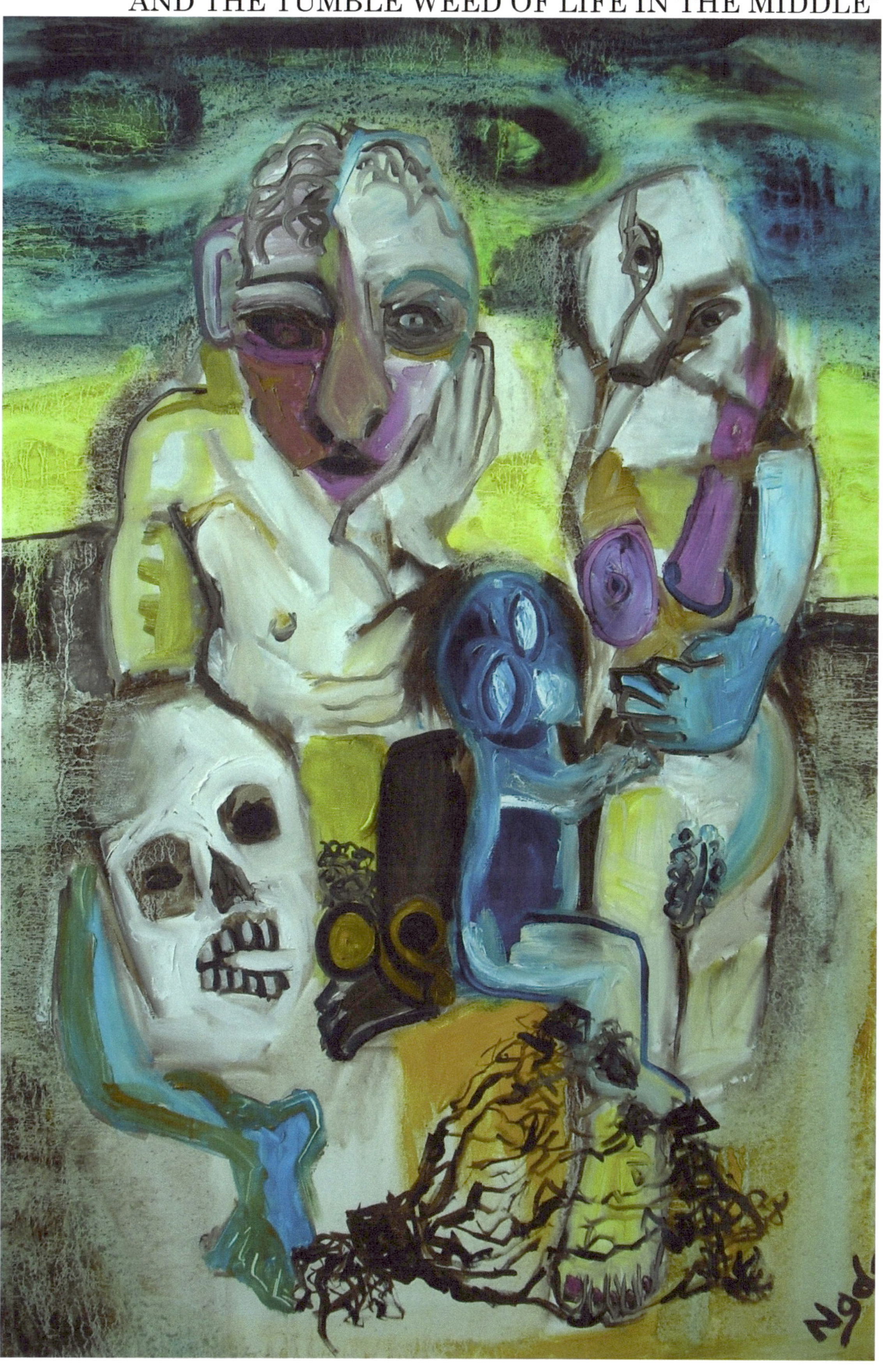

Technique: Oil painting on canvas - Size: 70 cm x 100 cm - Year: 2015

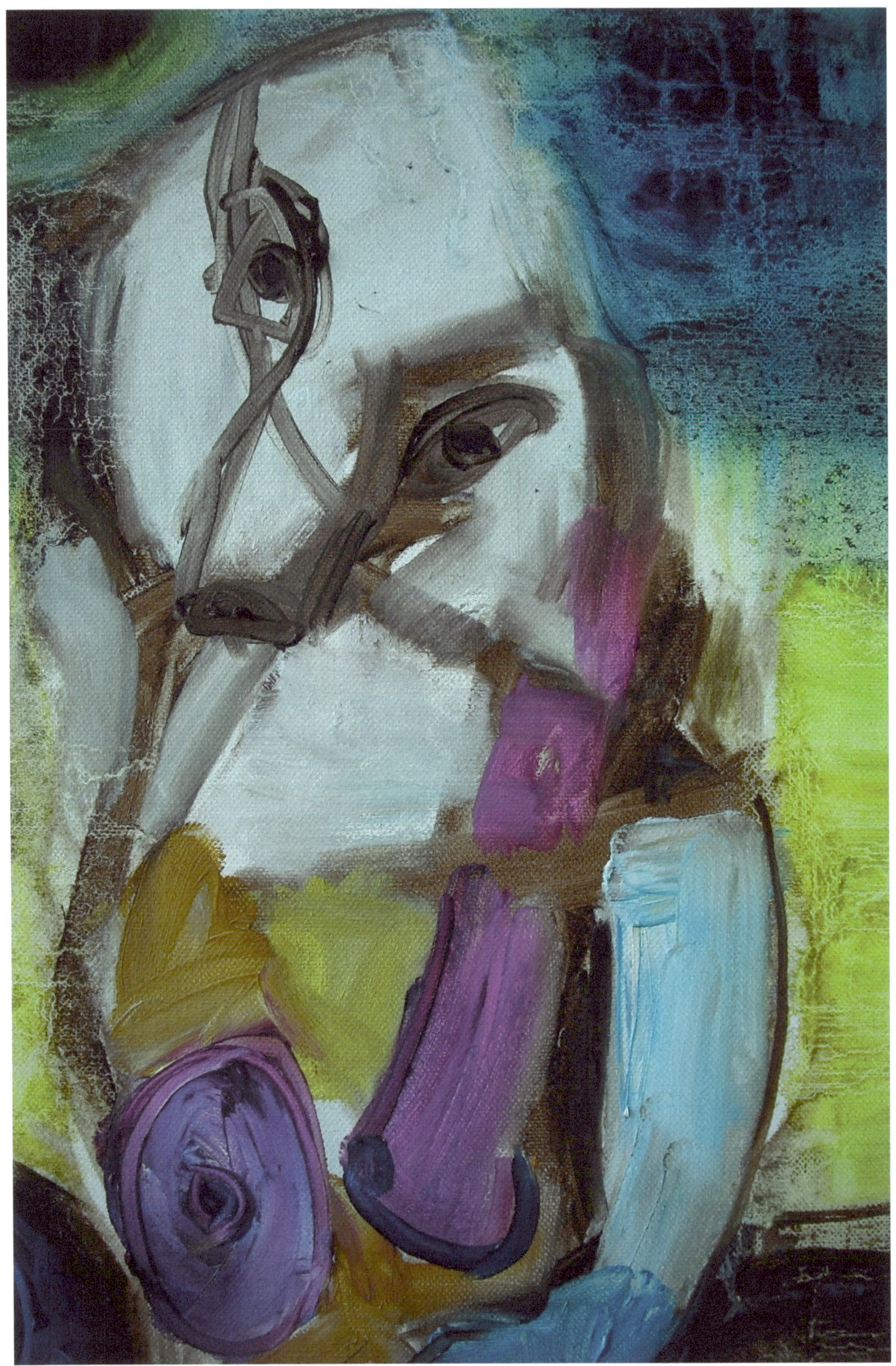

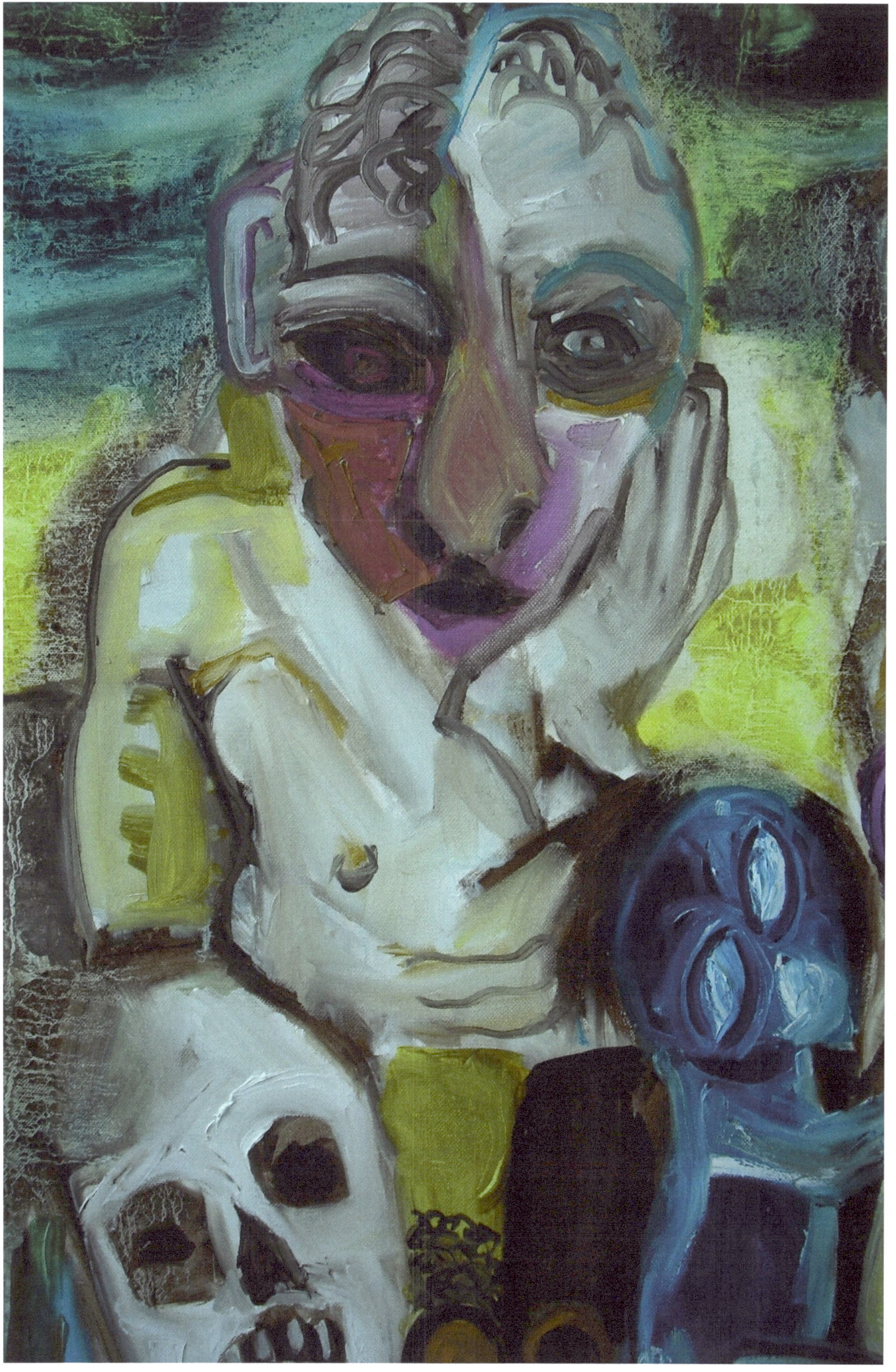

"ALBINO GIRL WITH MOTHER BESIDE A DEAD TREE, NEAR MOSHI, TANZANIA"

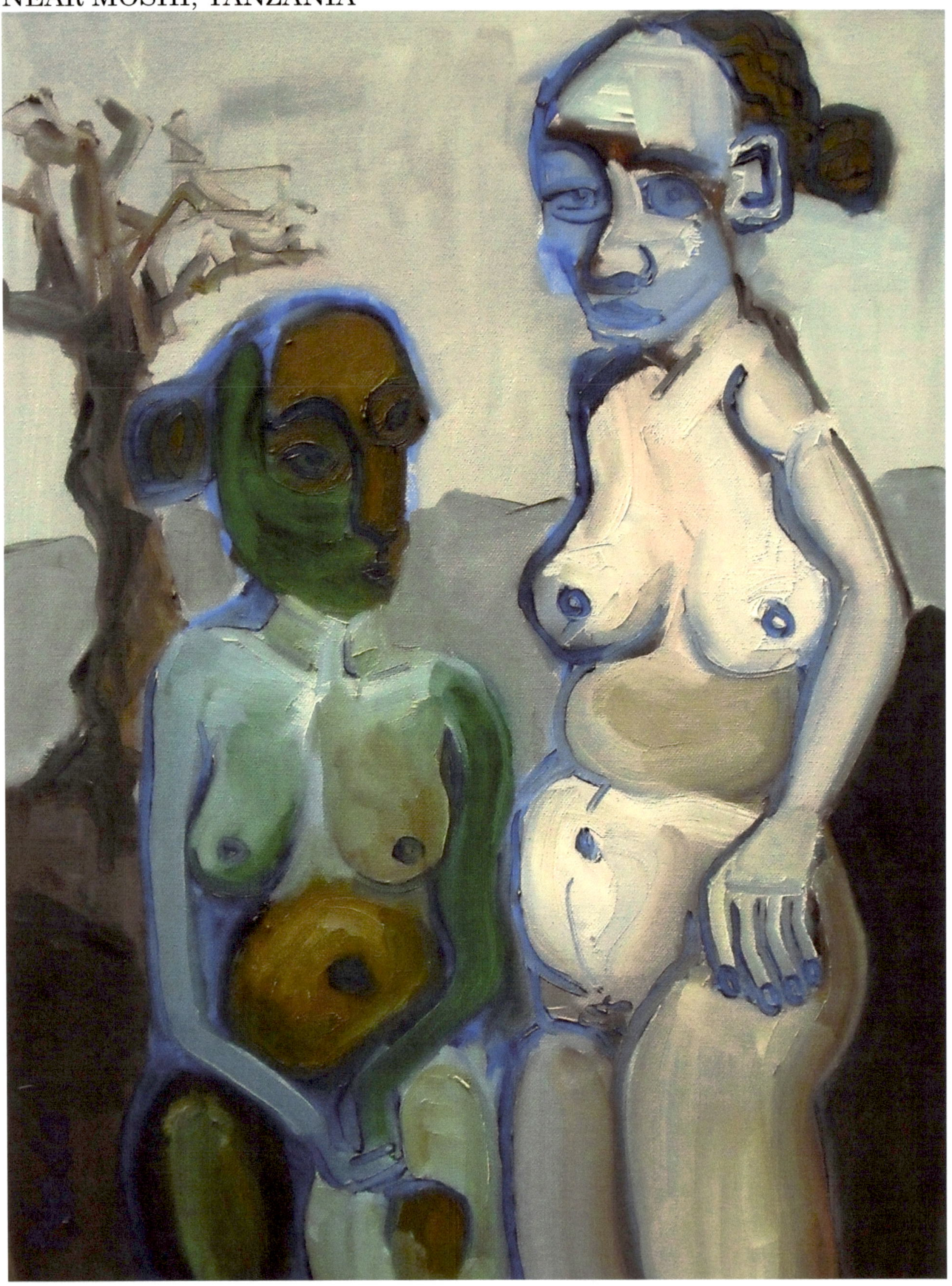

Technique: Oil painting on canvas
Size: 60 cm x 40 cm - Year: 2015

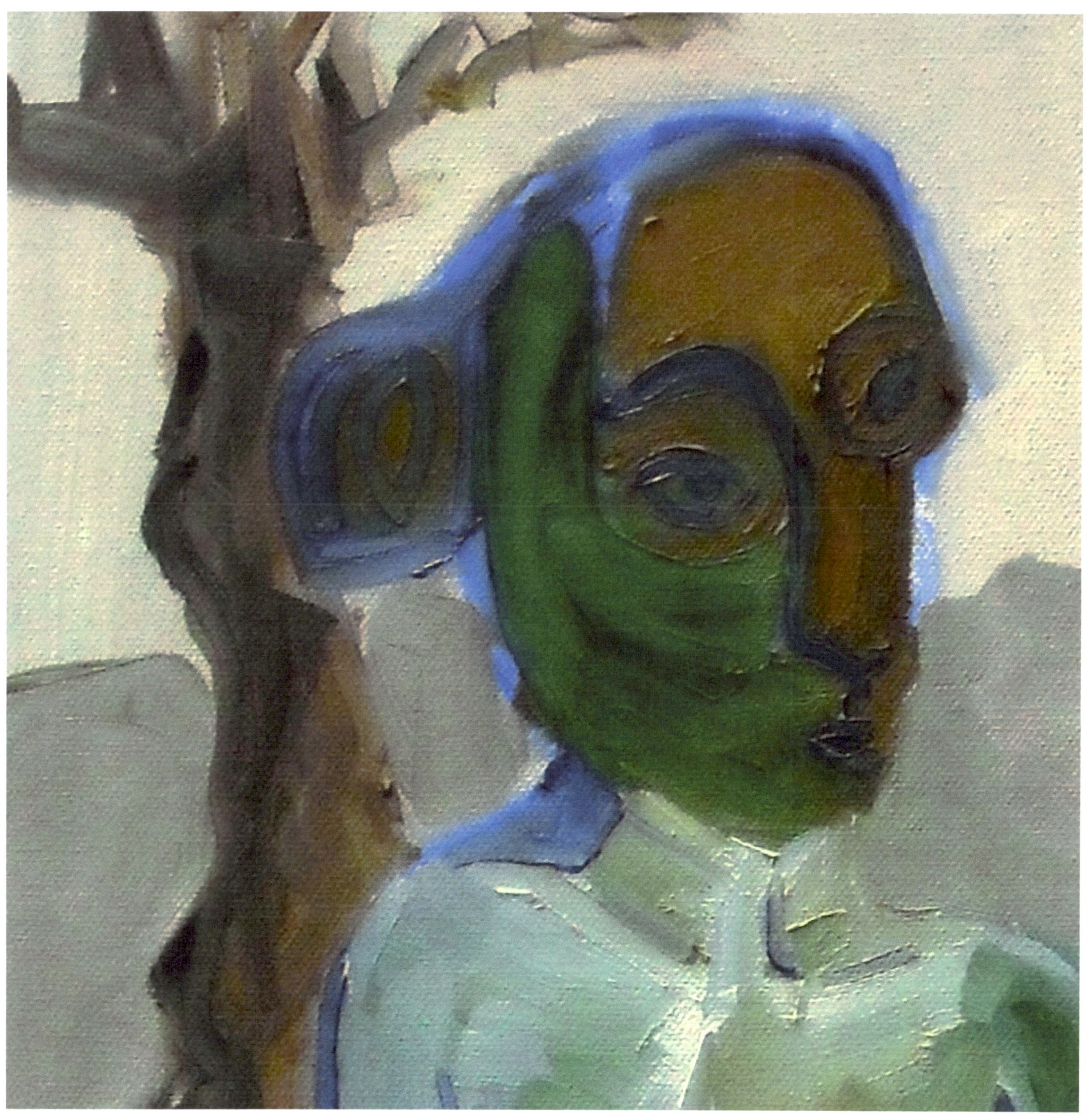

Detail 2

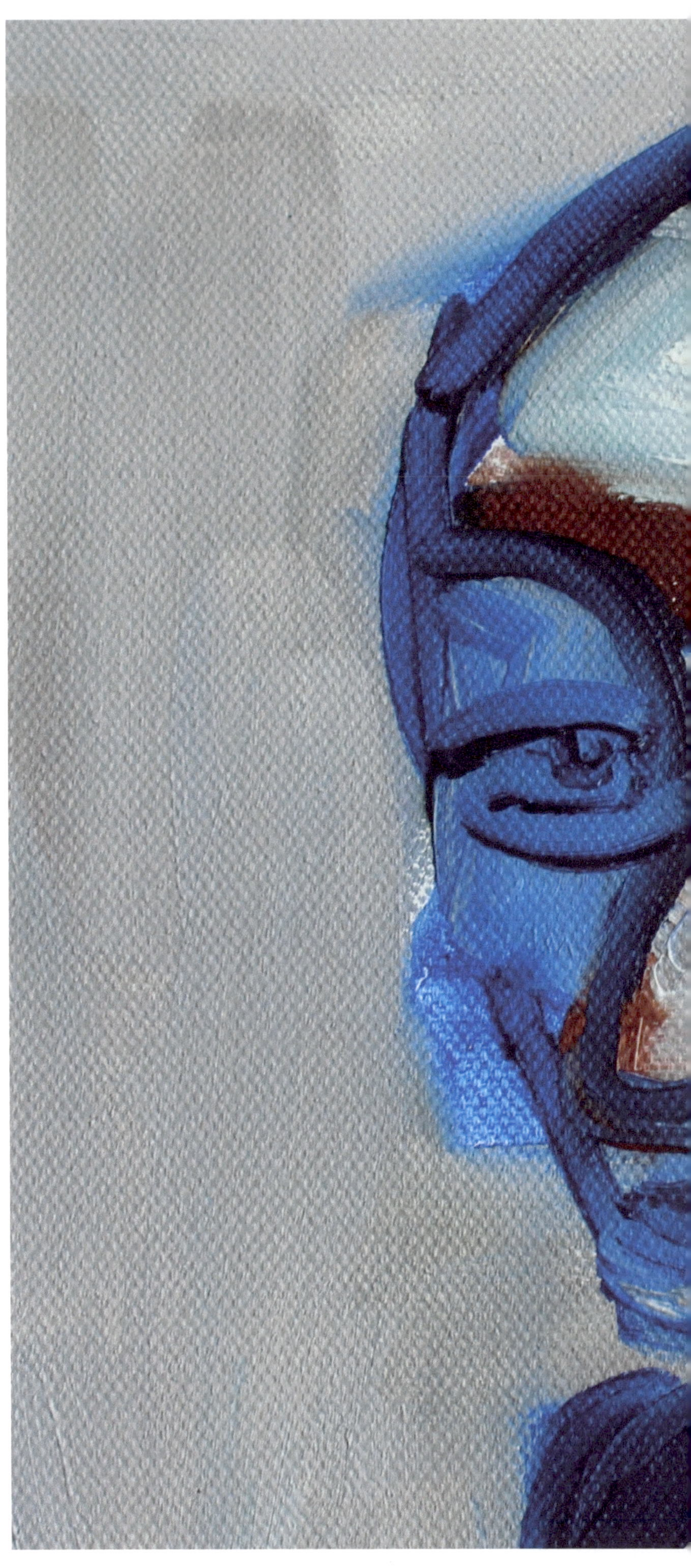

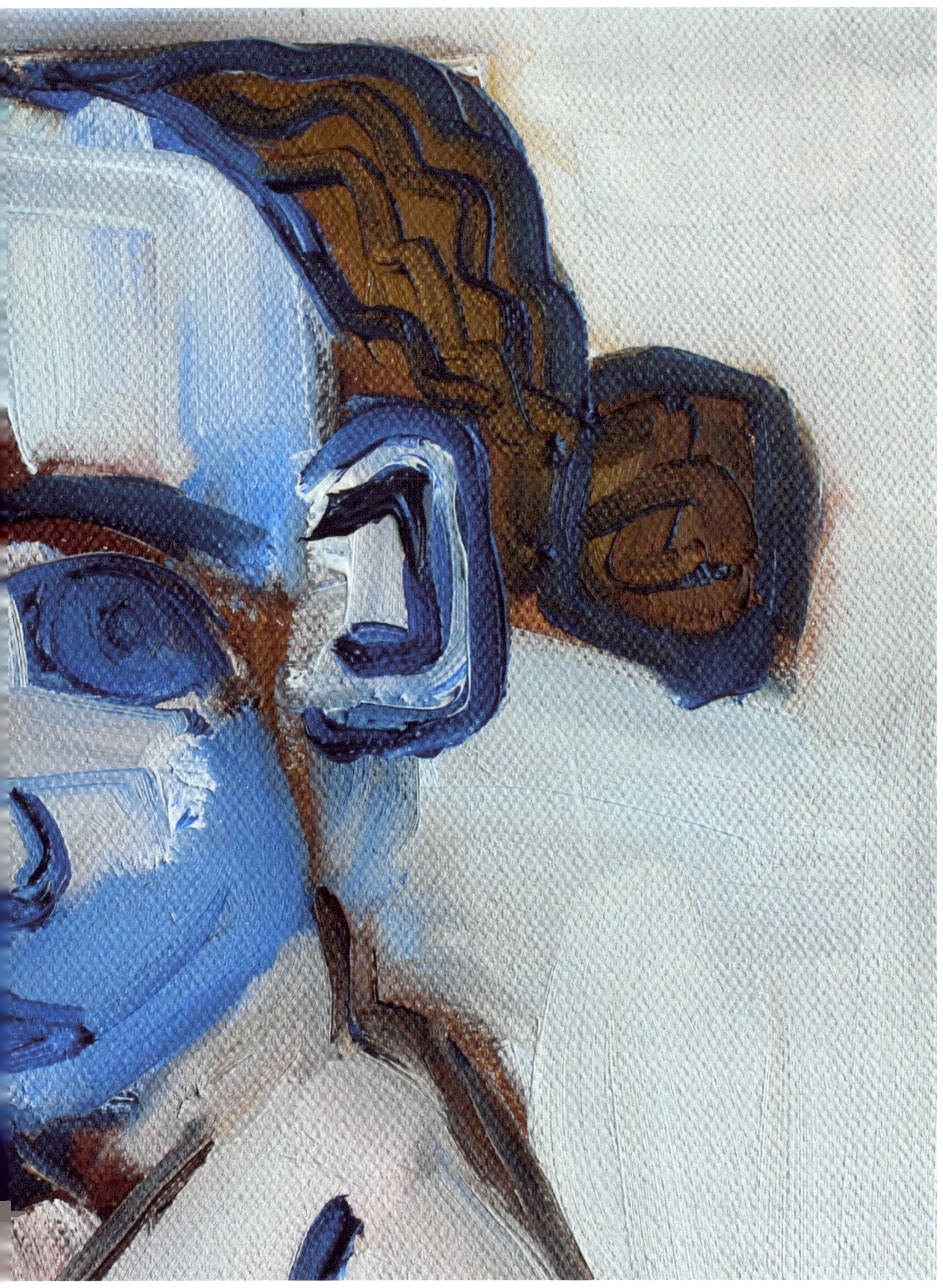

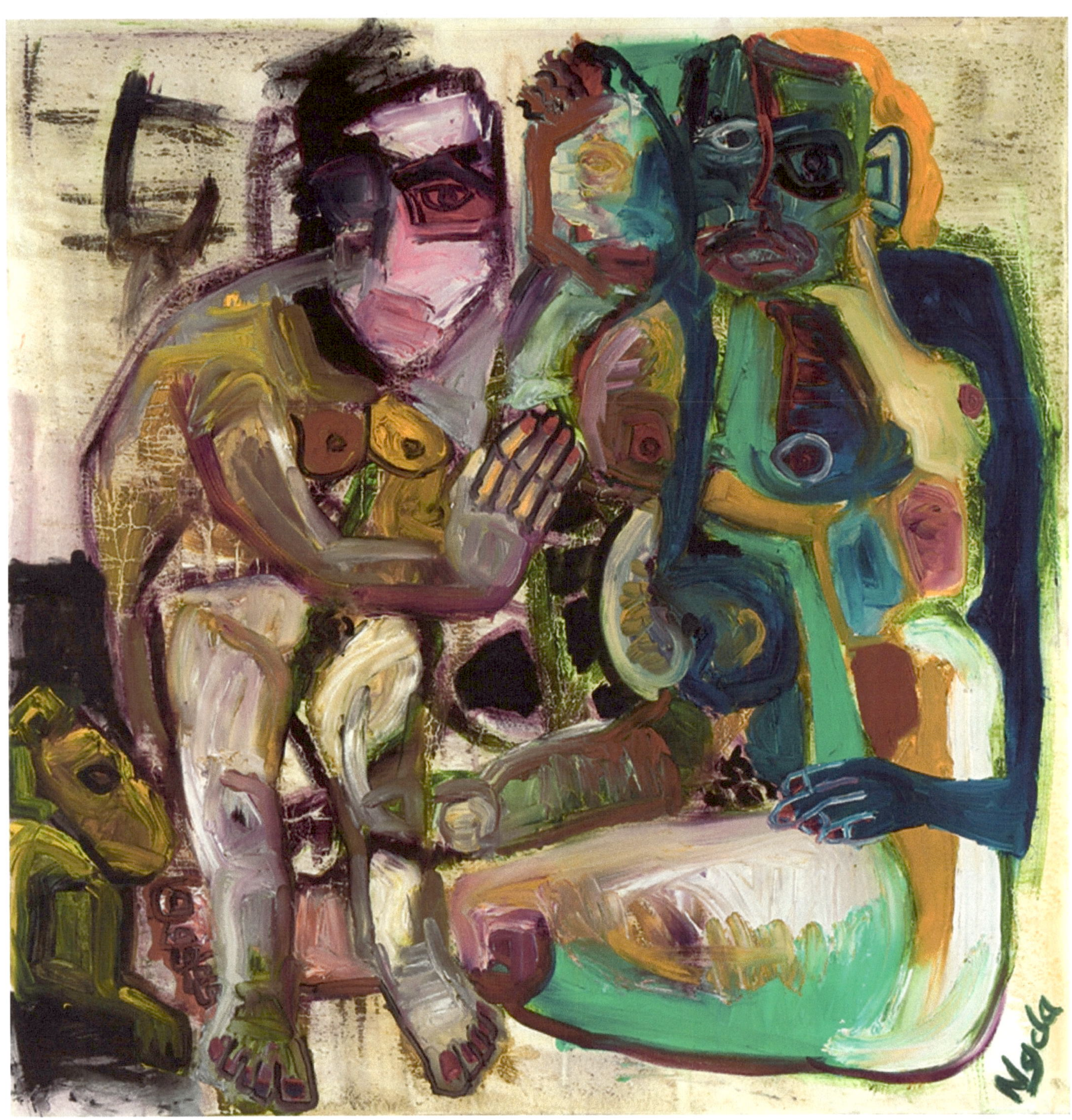

Technique: Oil painting on canvas
Size: 80 cm x 80 cm
Year: 2015

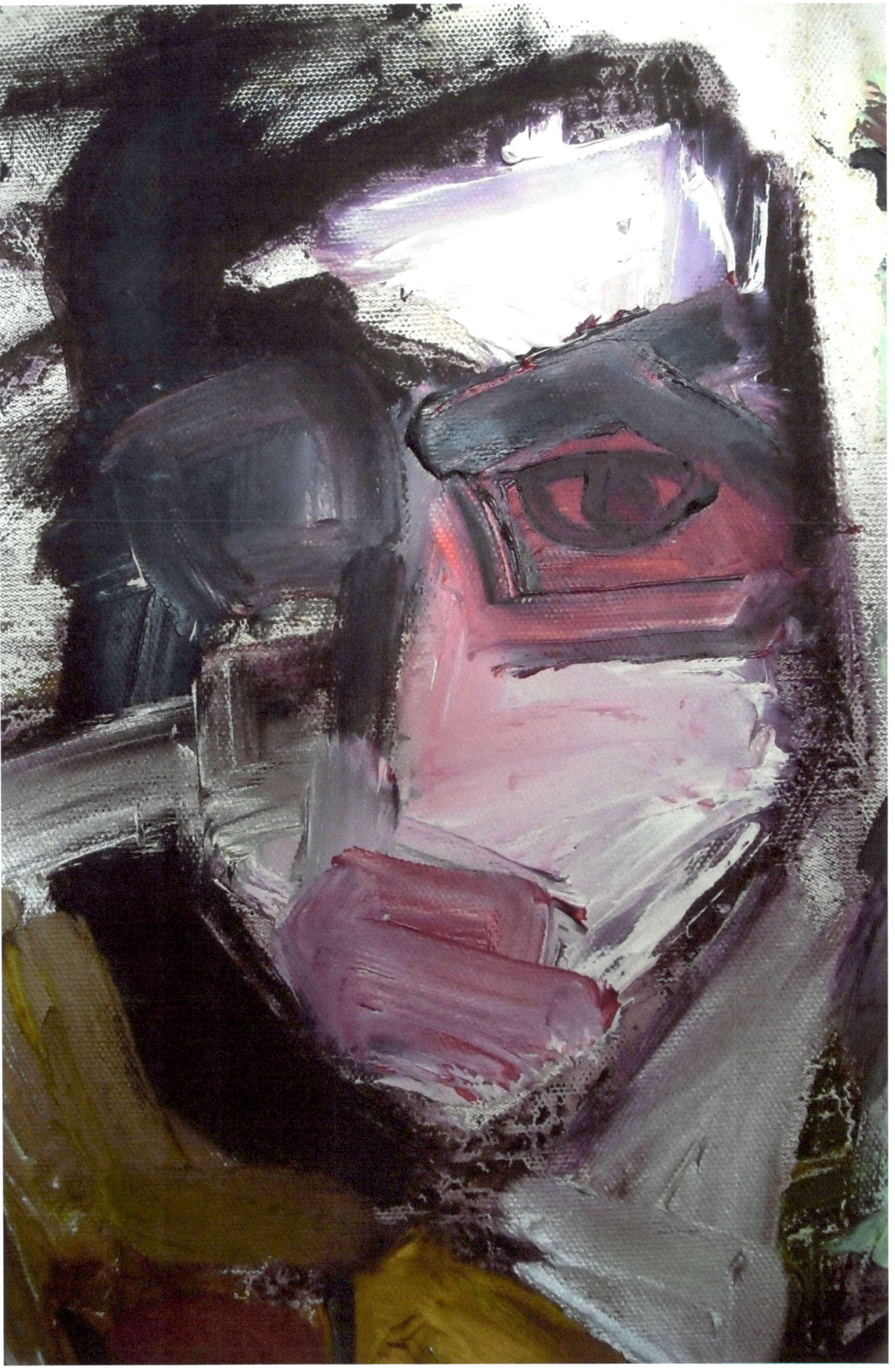

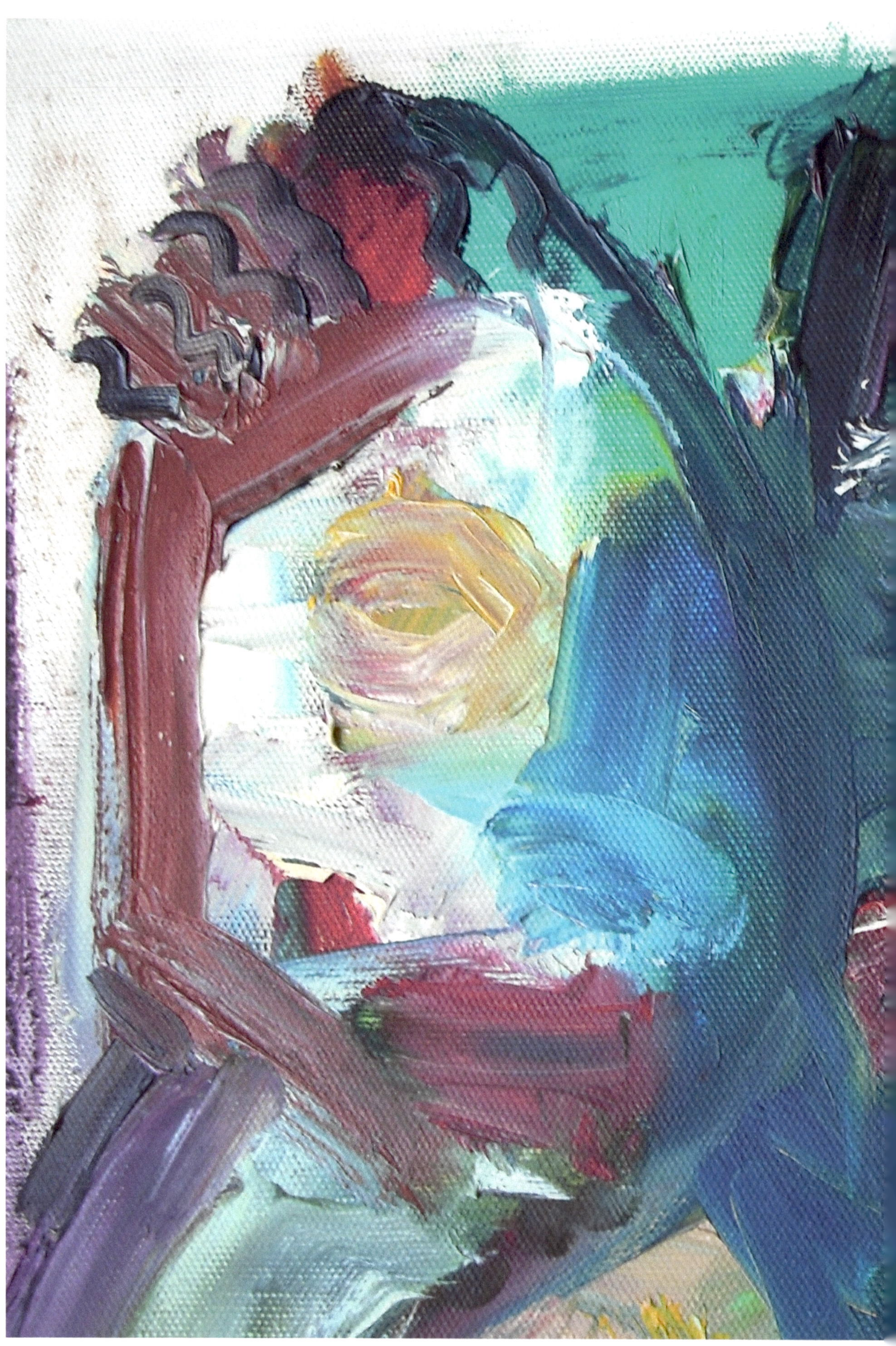

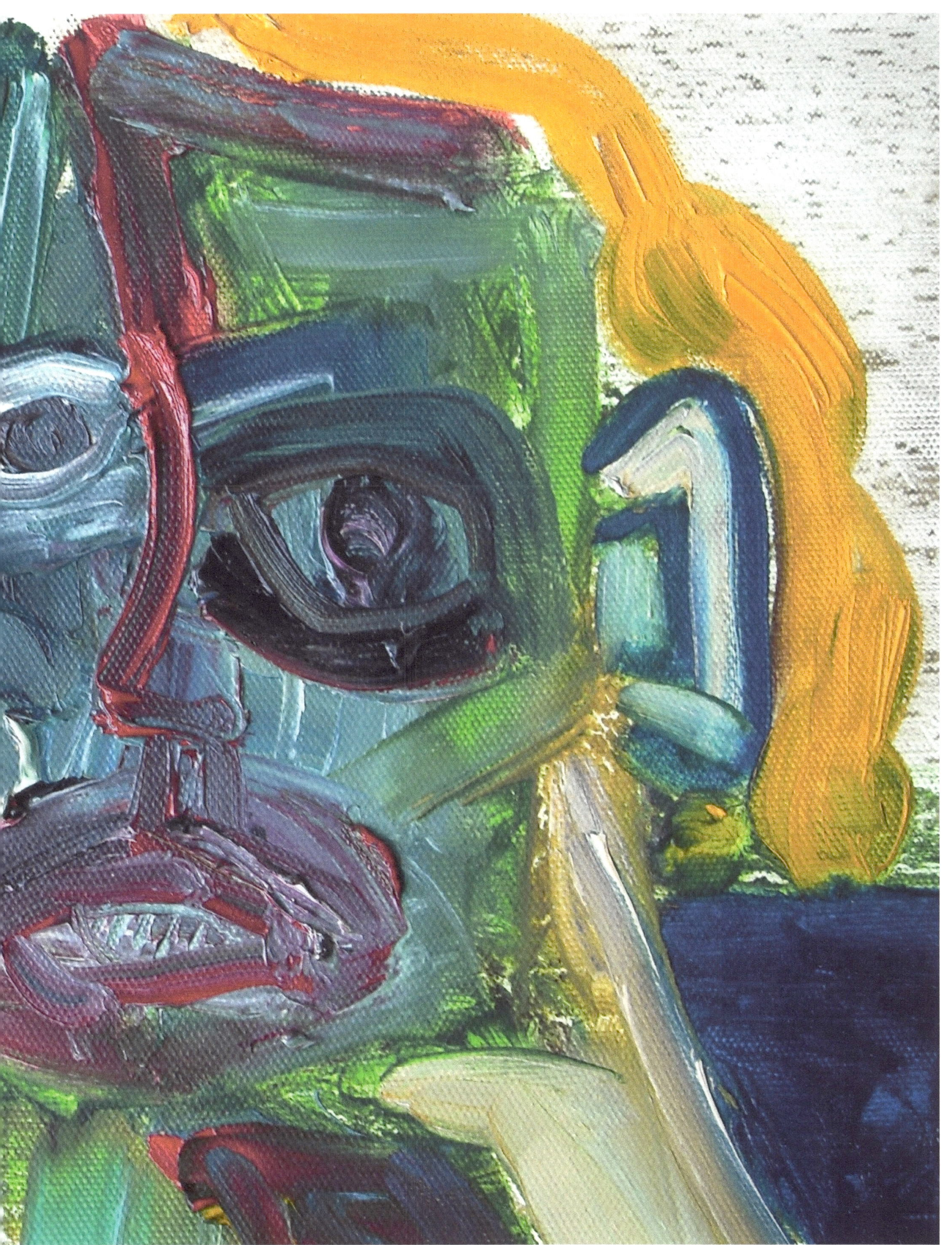

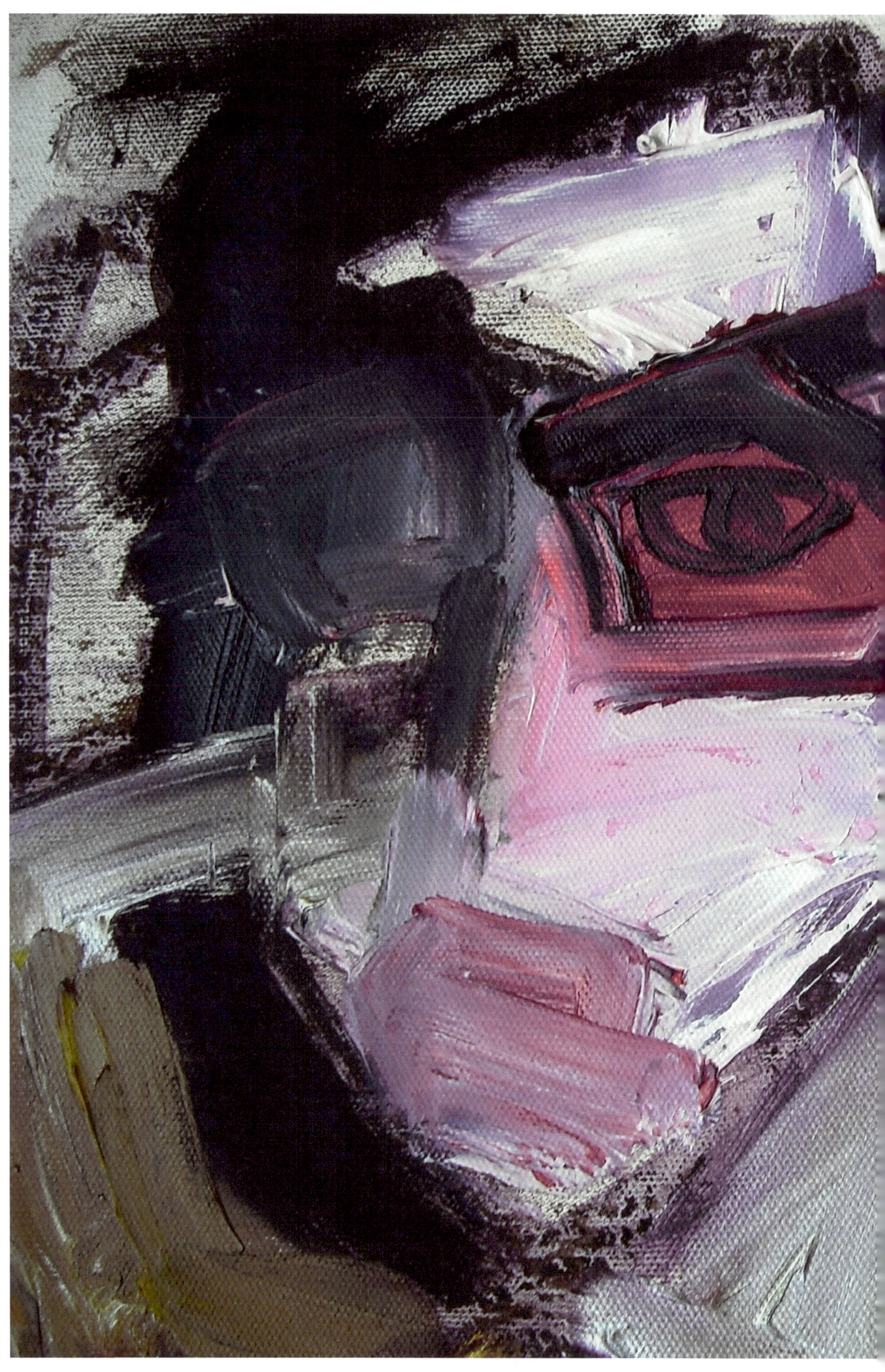

Detail 3

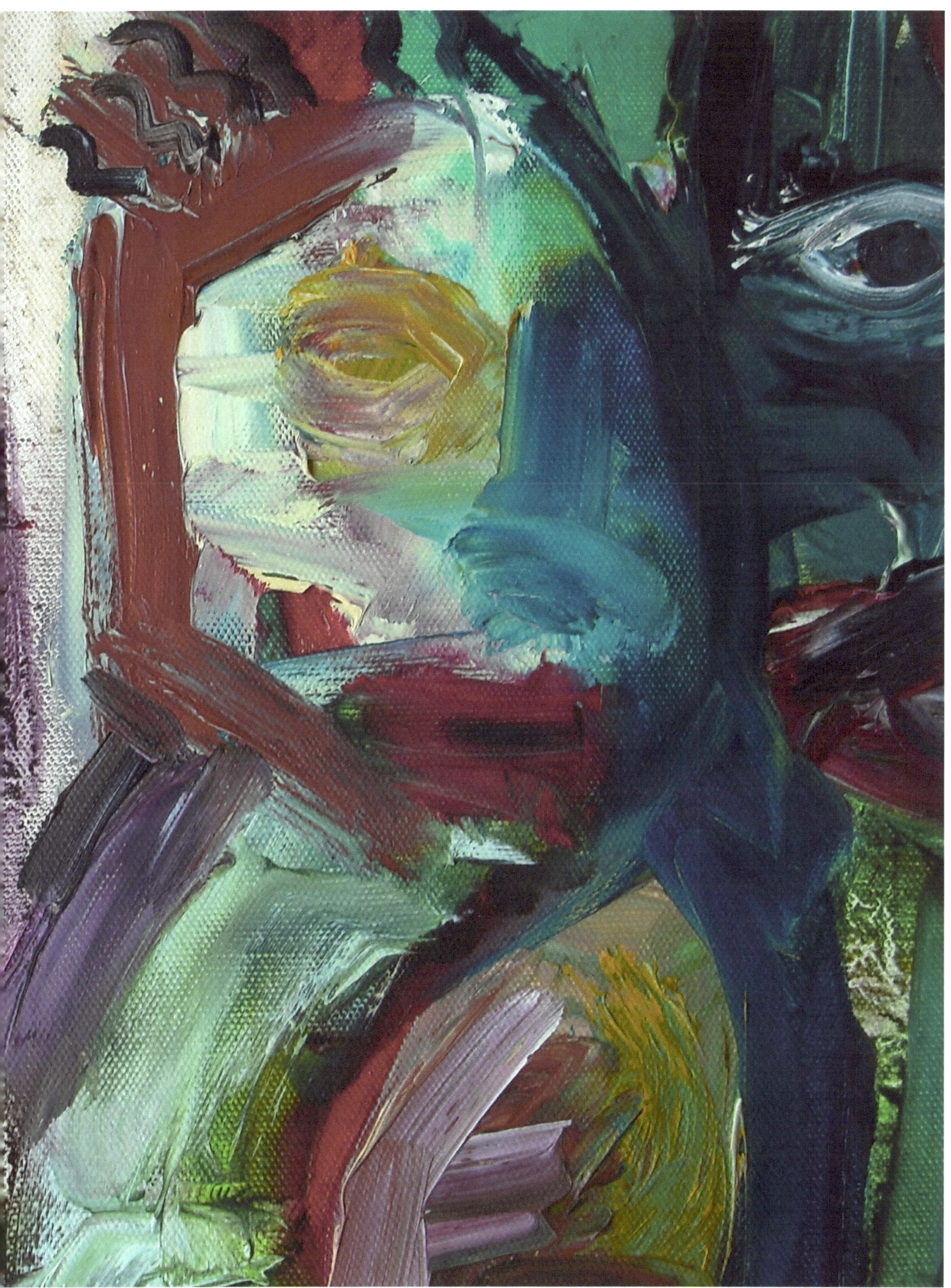

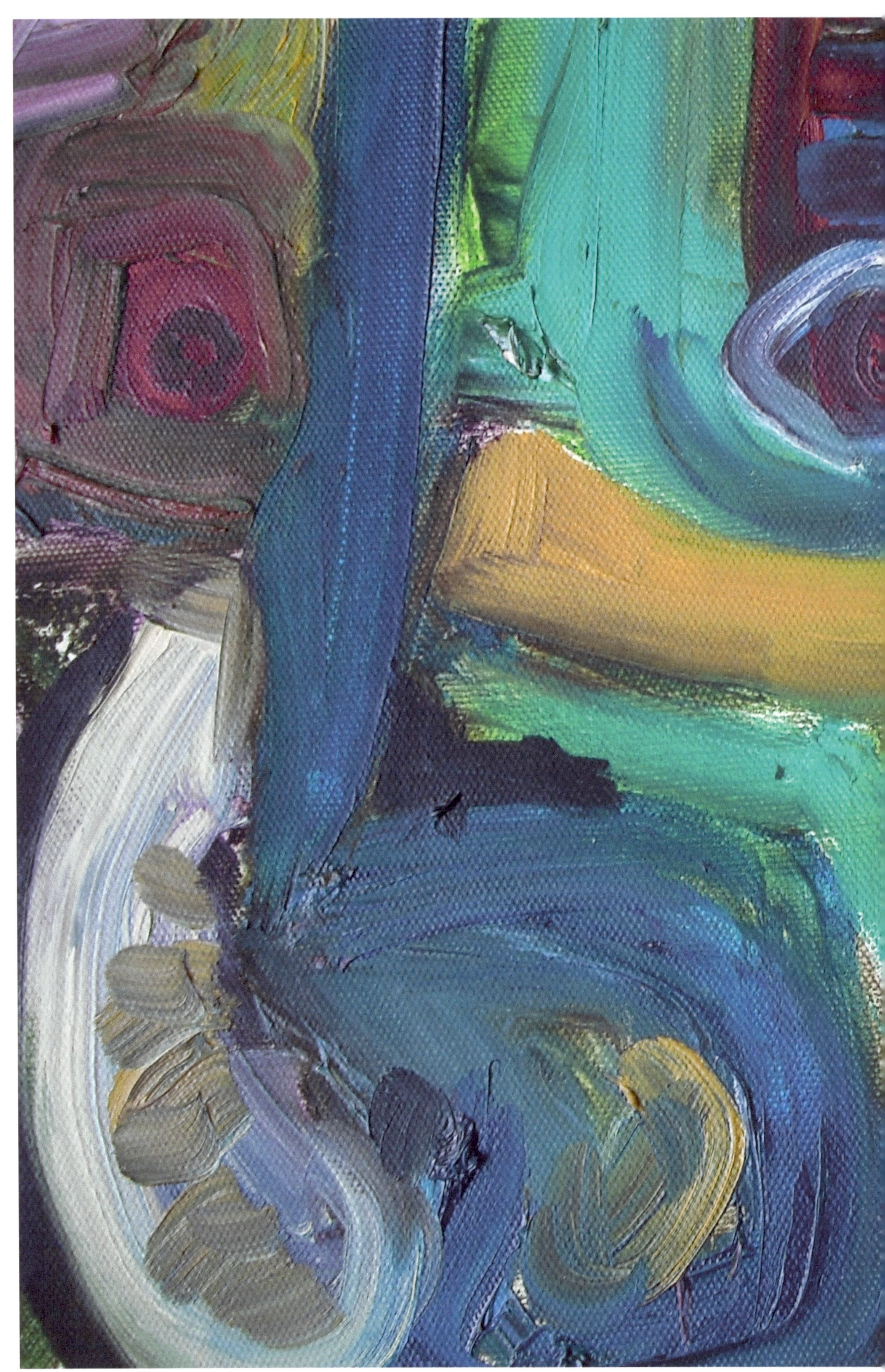

Detail 4

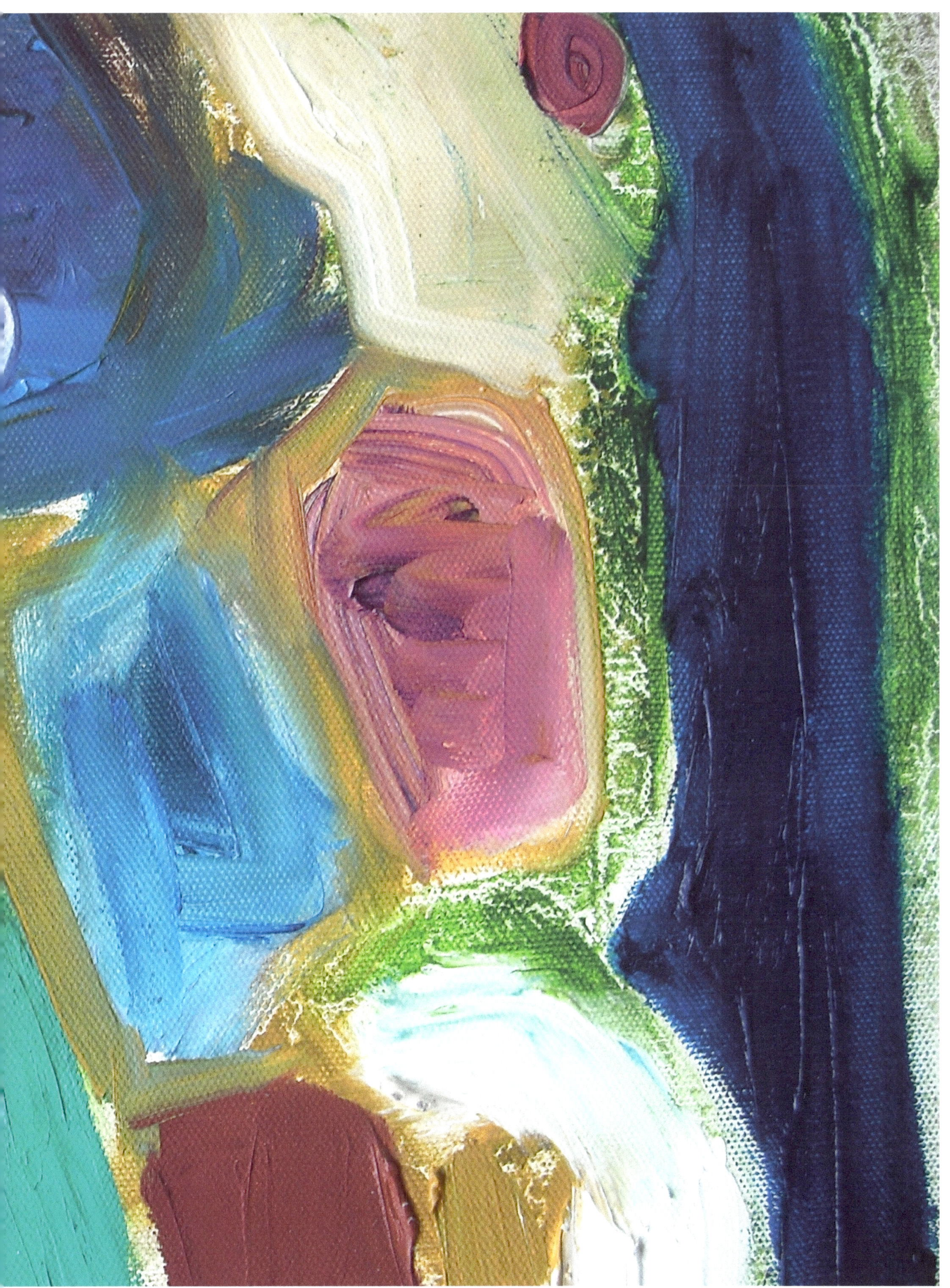

Detail 5

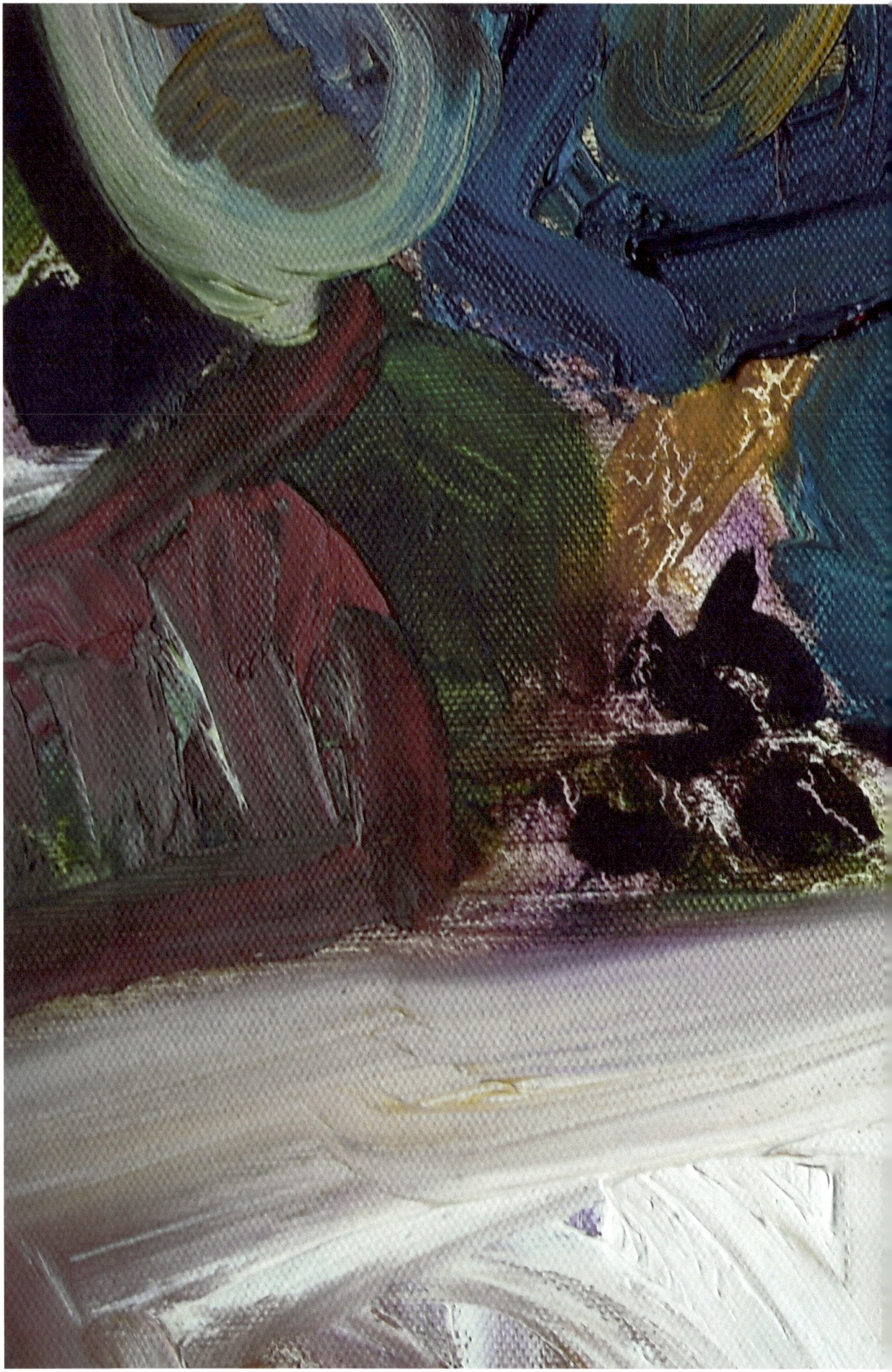

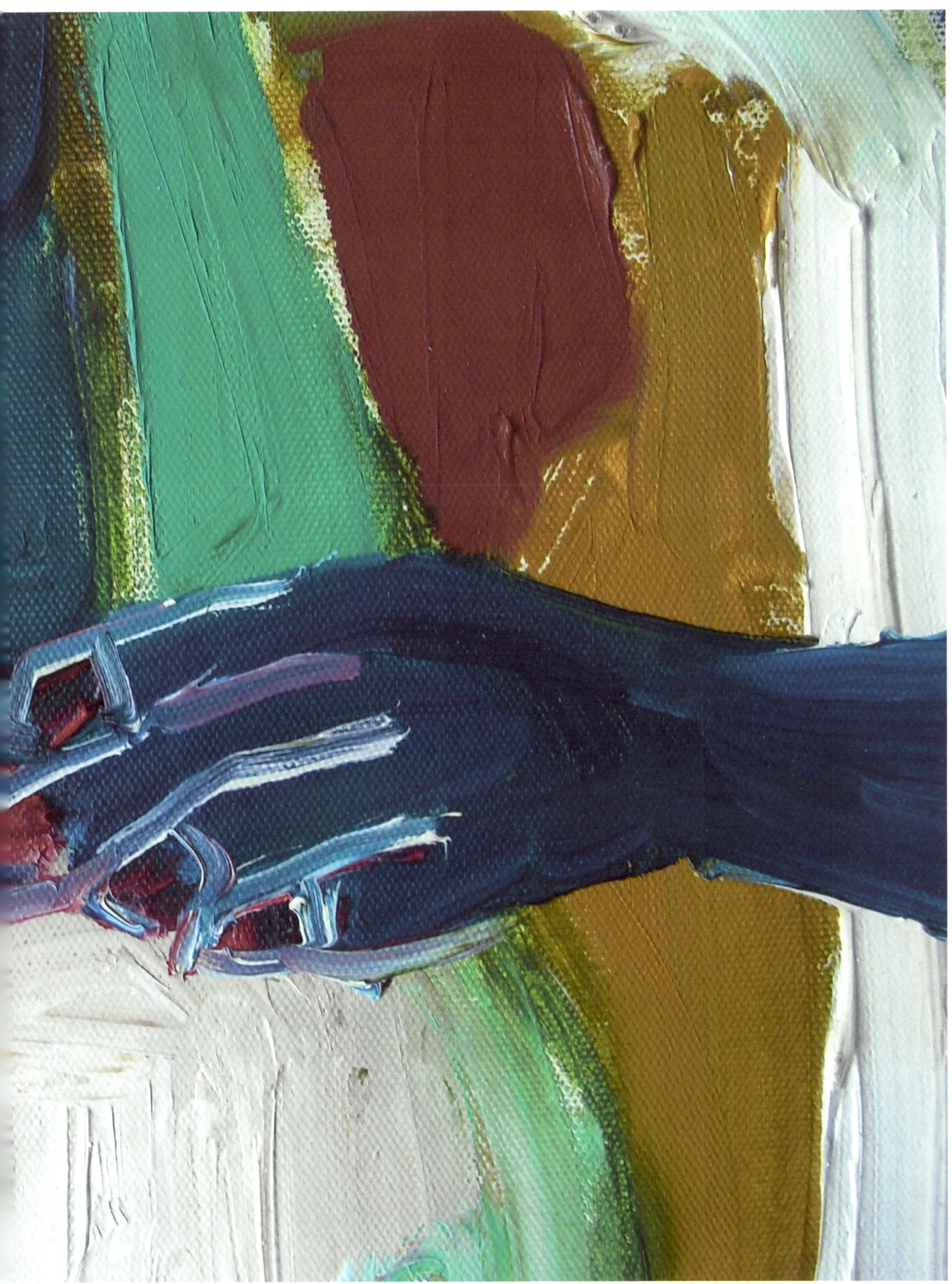

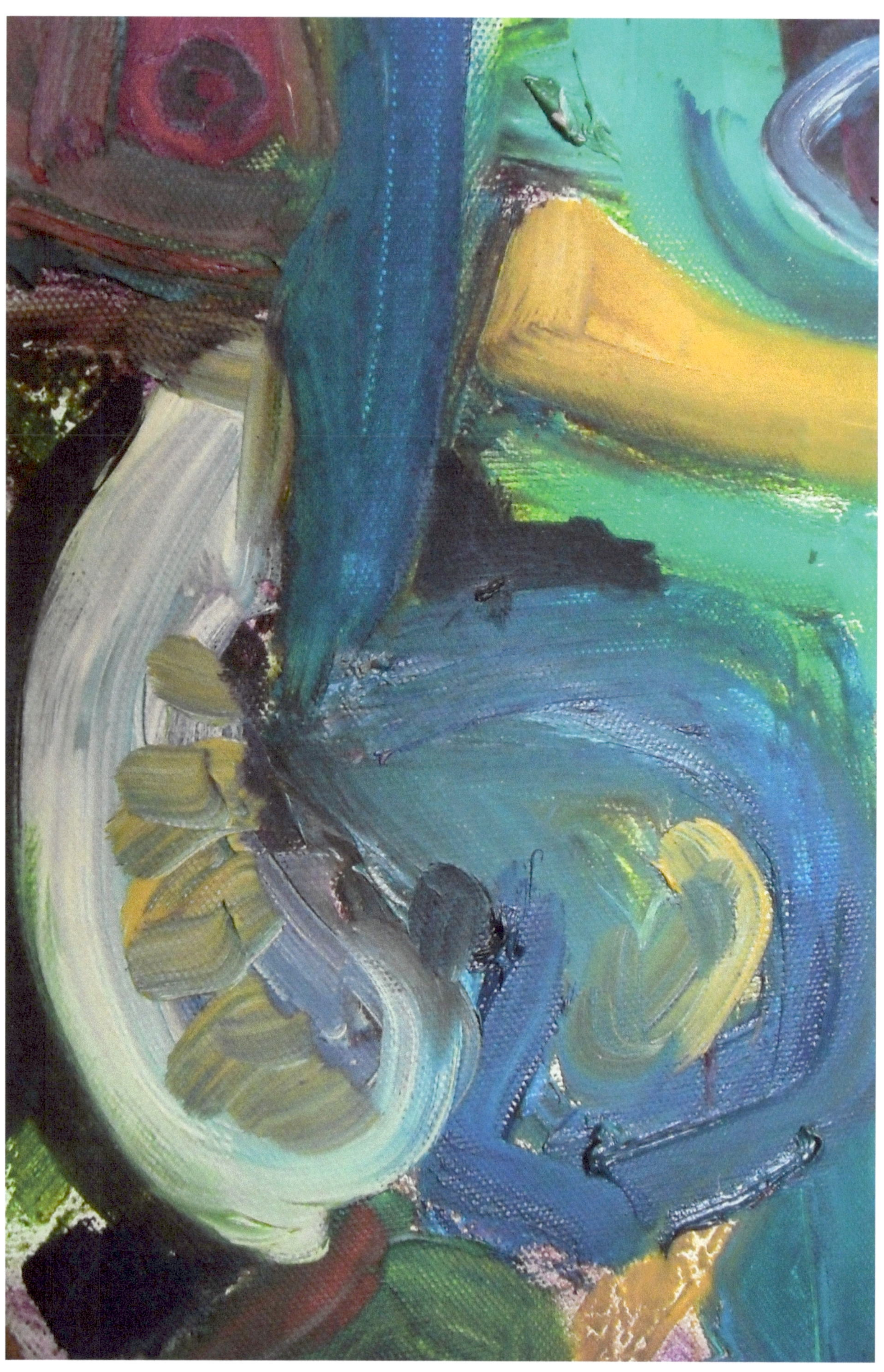

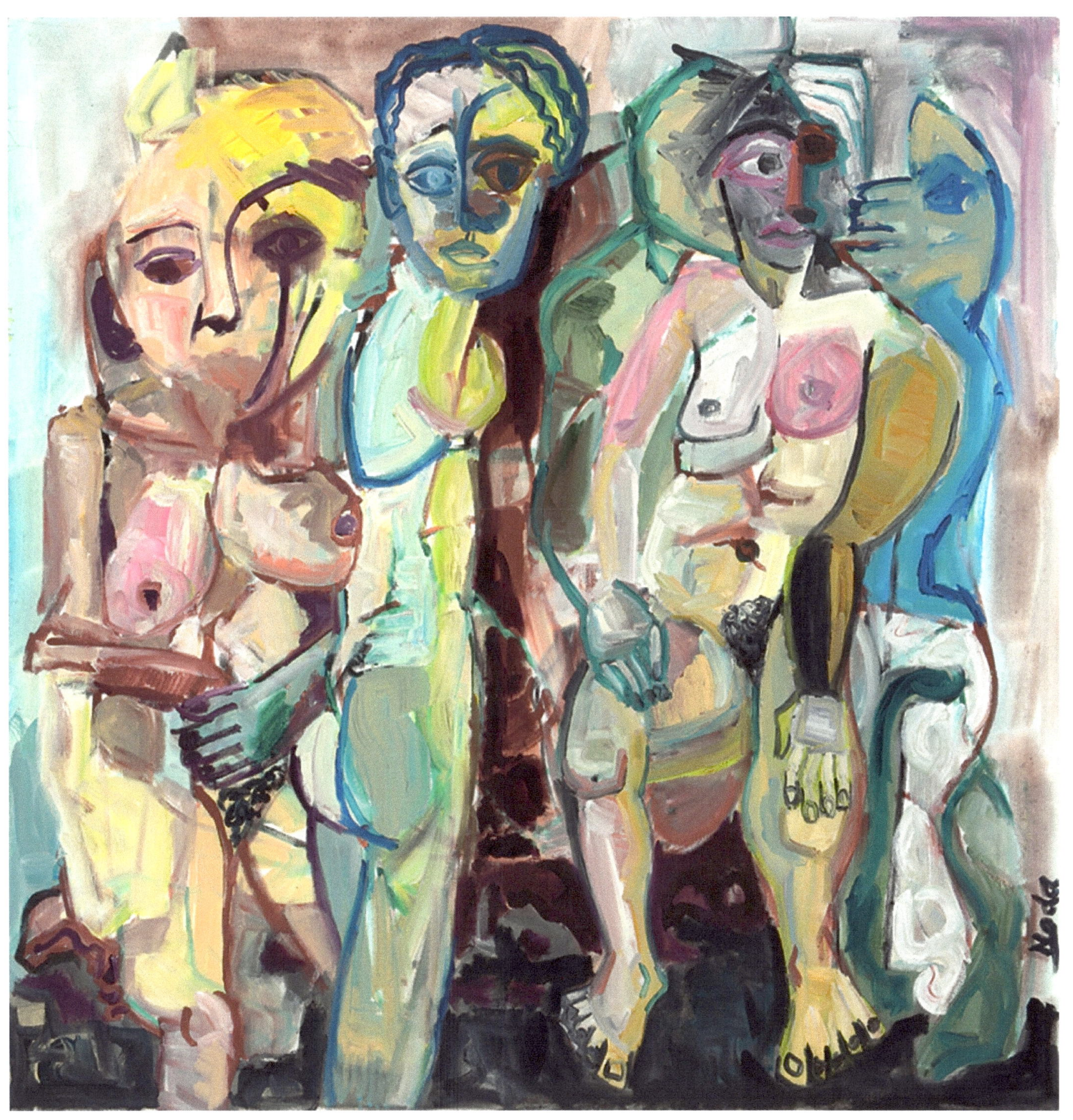

Technique: Oil painting on canvas
Size: 80 cm x 80 cm
Year: 2015

Detail 1

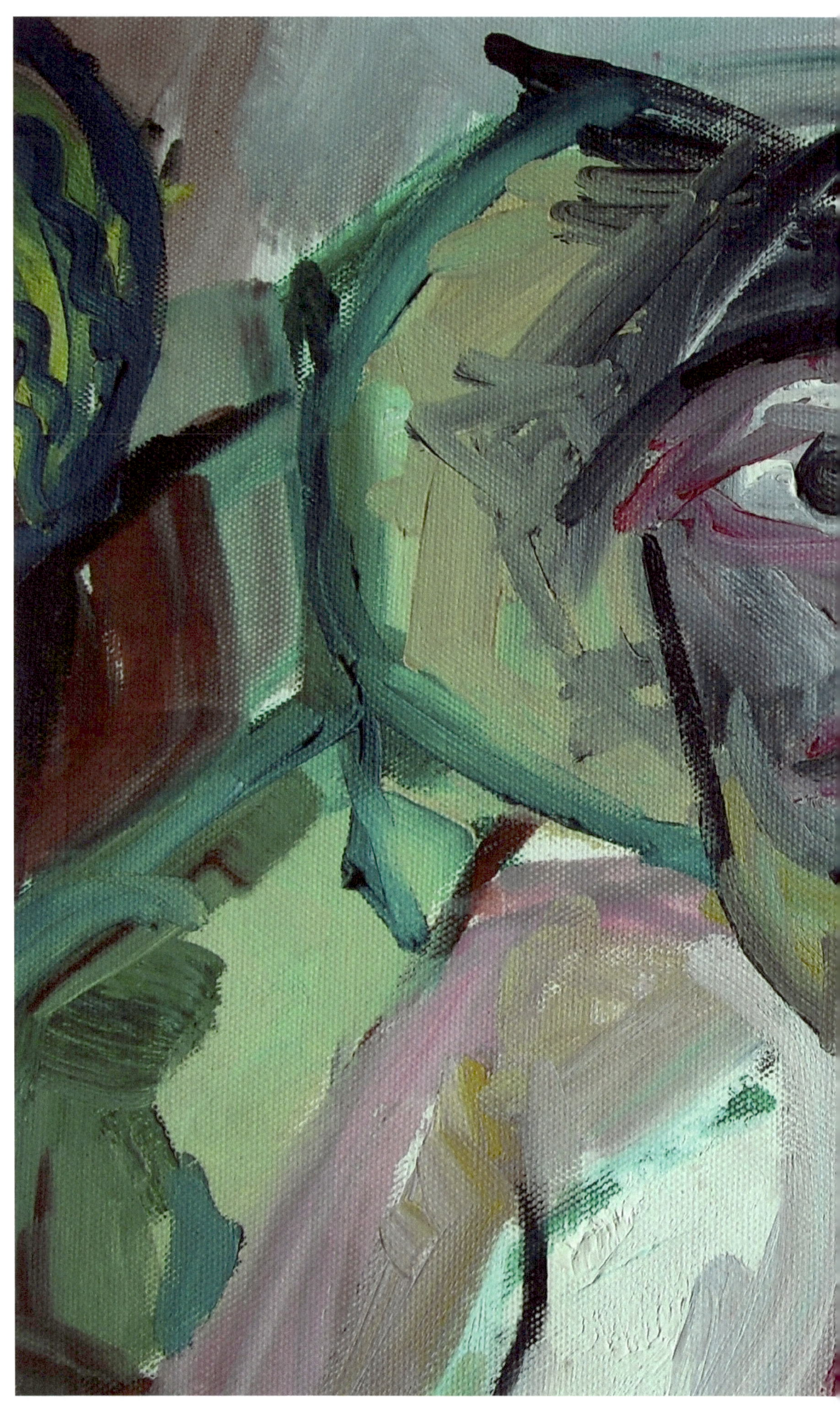

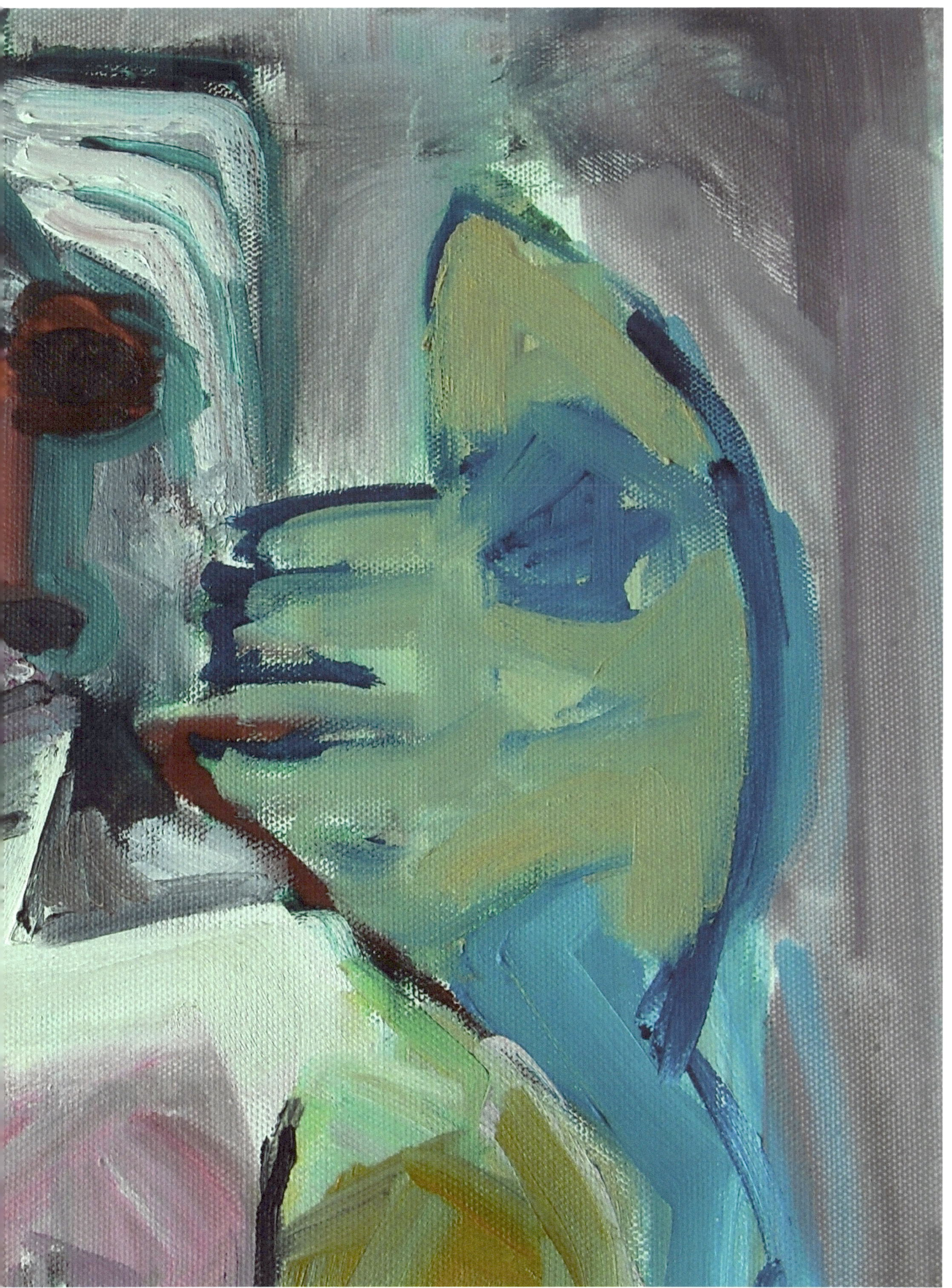

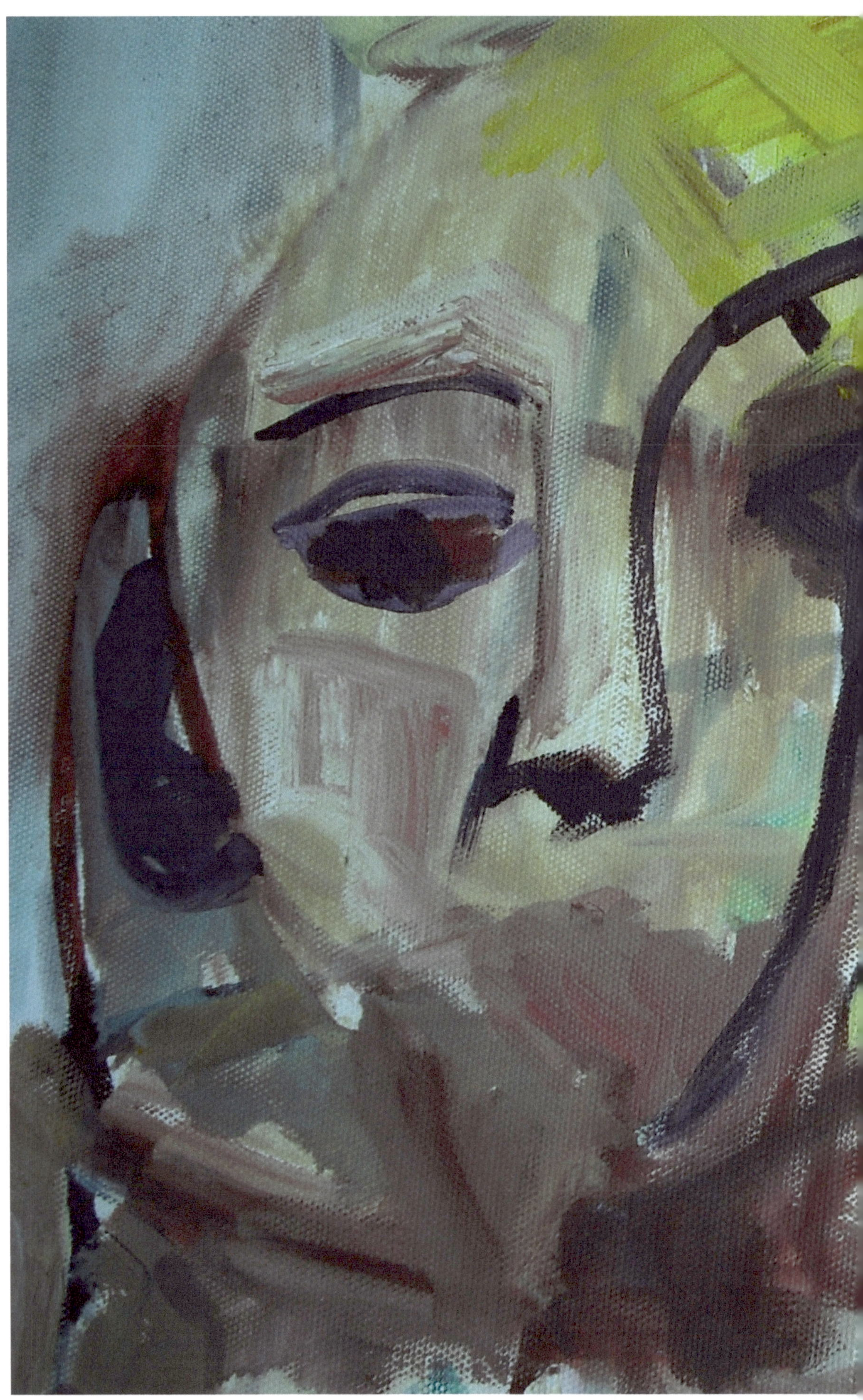

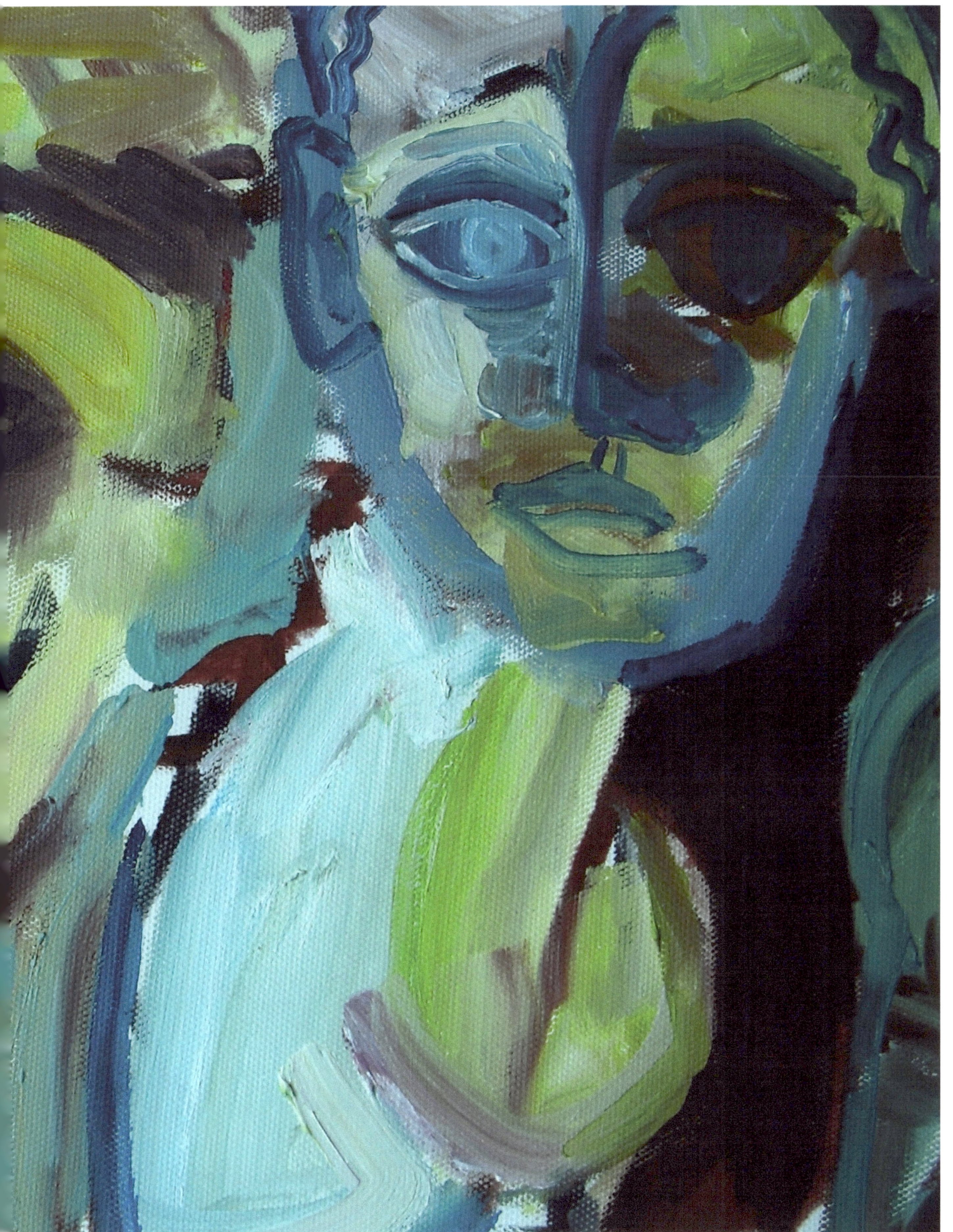

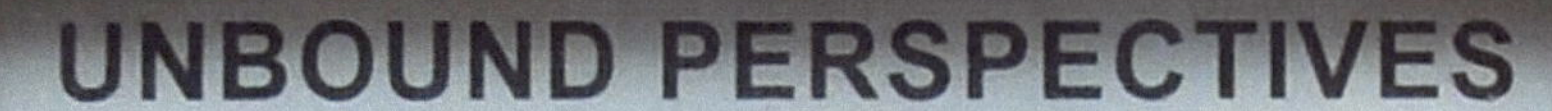

UNBOUND PERSPECTIVES

June 10 - June 30, 2017
Reception: Thursday June 15, 2017 6-8 PM

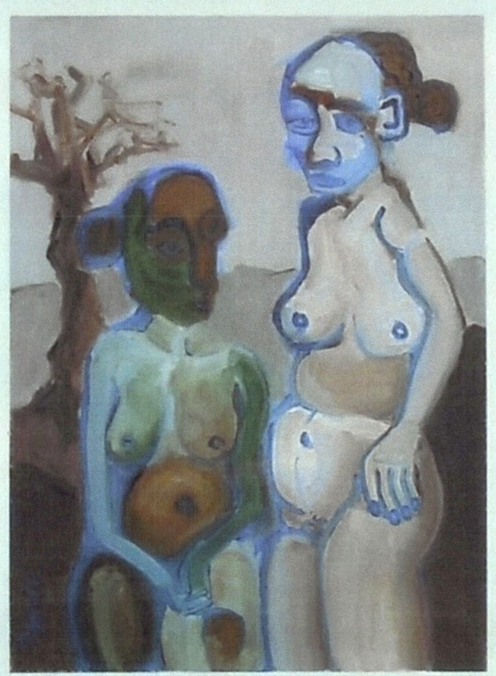

© Stephen Najda, *Albino Woman with Mother Beside a Dead Tree, Near Moshi, Tanzania*, Oil on Canvas, 25.5" x 19.5"

Alexander Adam | Carmen Félix | Claudia C Forero | Gita Levy
Máribel Matthews | Vinod More | Stephen Najda | Shifra
Jolanta Talaikiene | Ken Wada | Saskia Weishut-Snapper
Josefina Wendel Carlsson | Johanna Wray

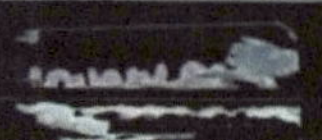

Agora Gallery

530 West 25th Street, New York, NY
www.Agora-Gallery.com

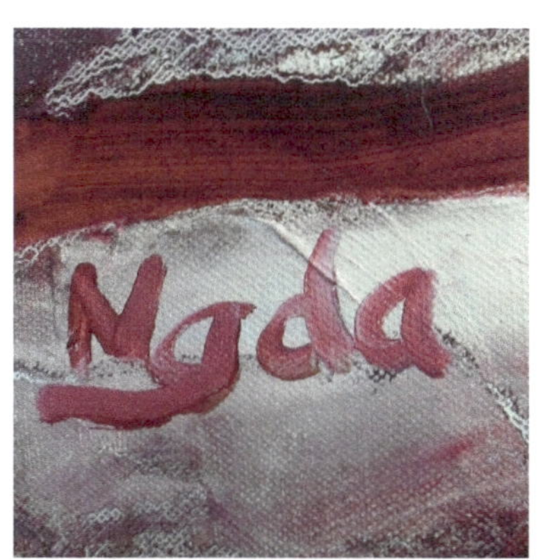

PHOTO GALLERY

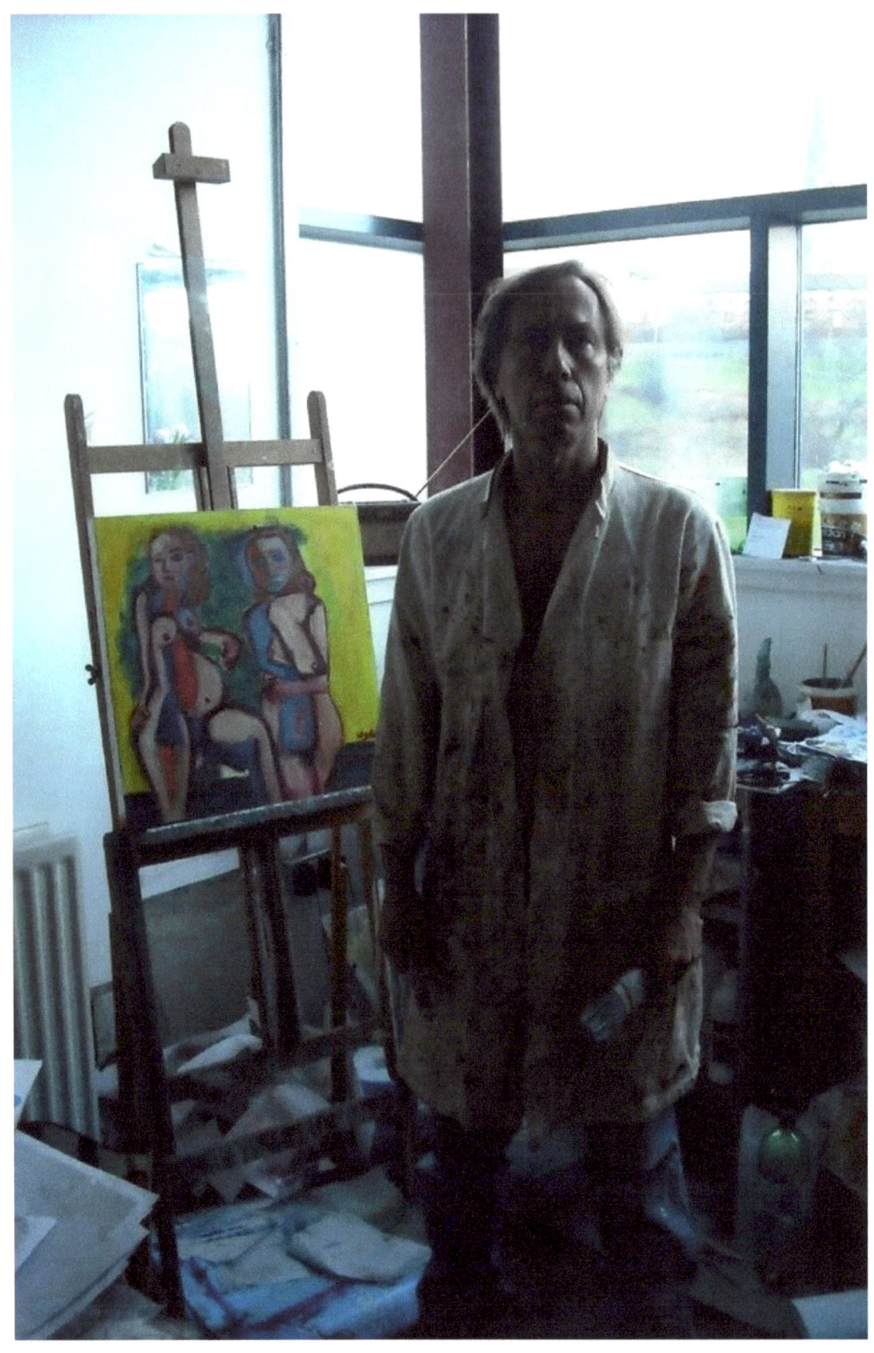

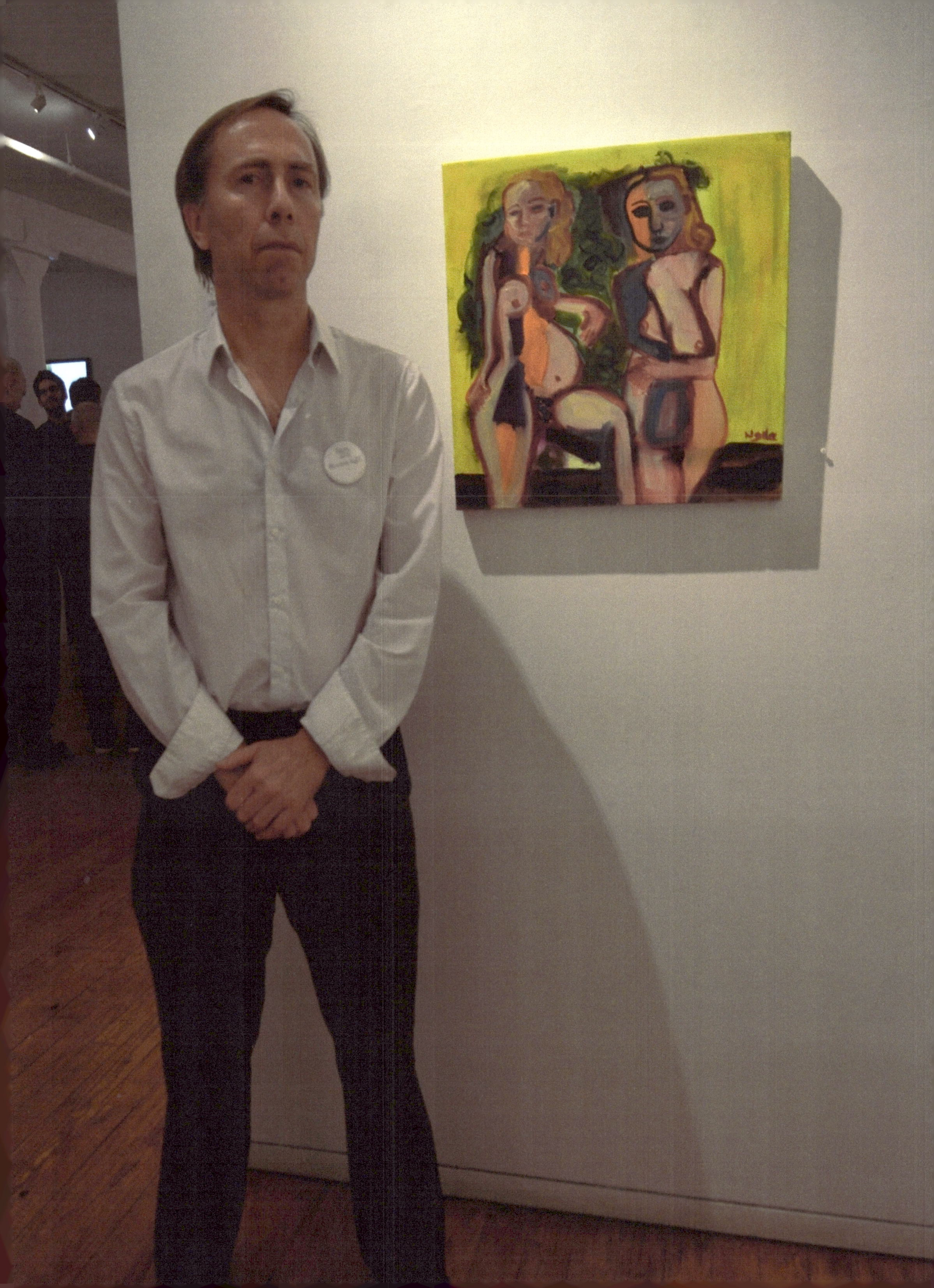

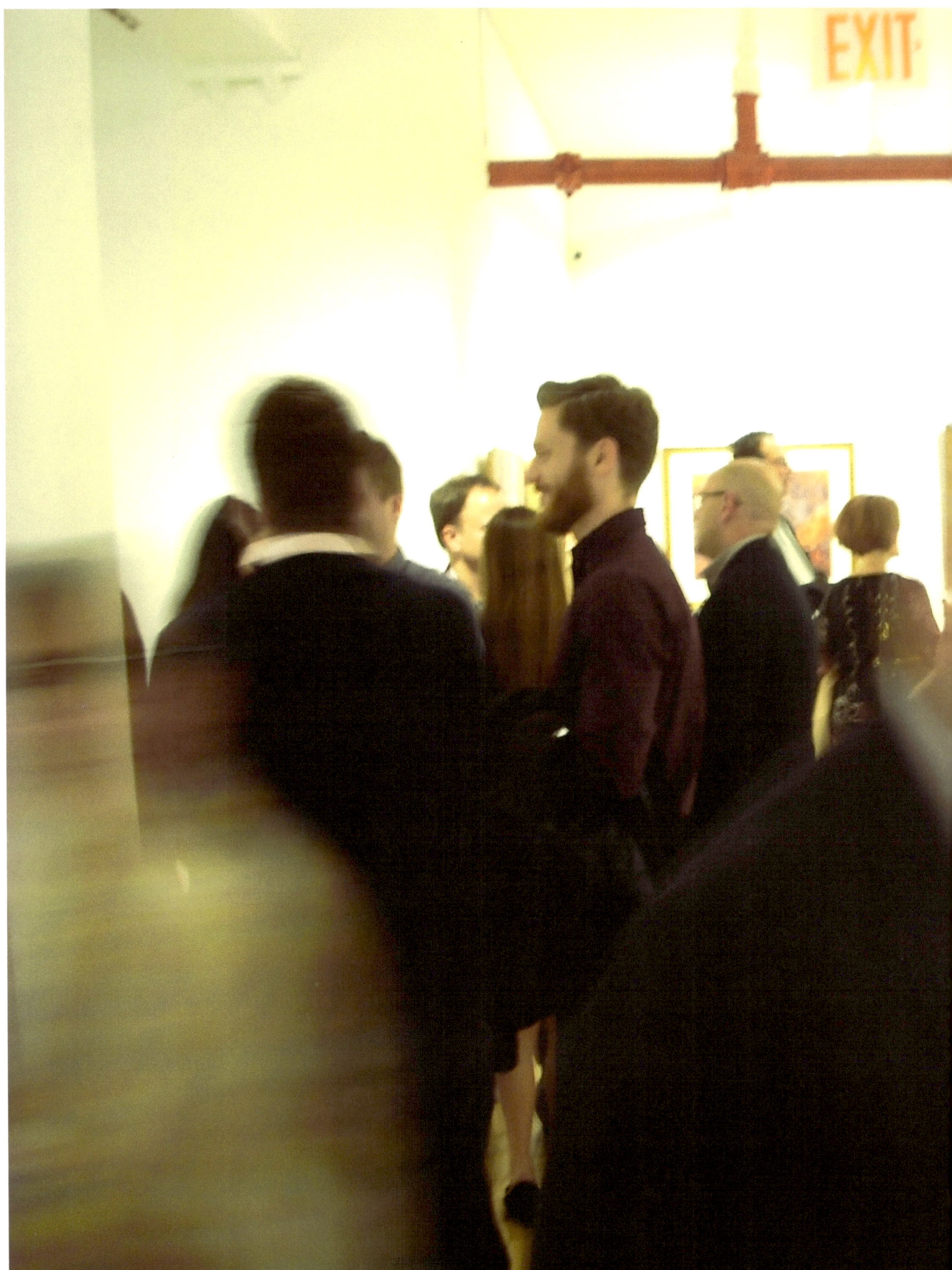

EXIT

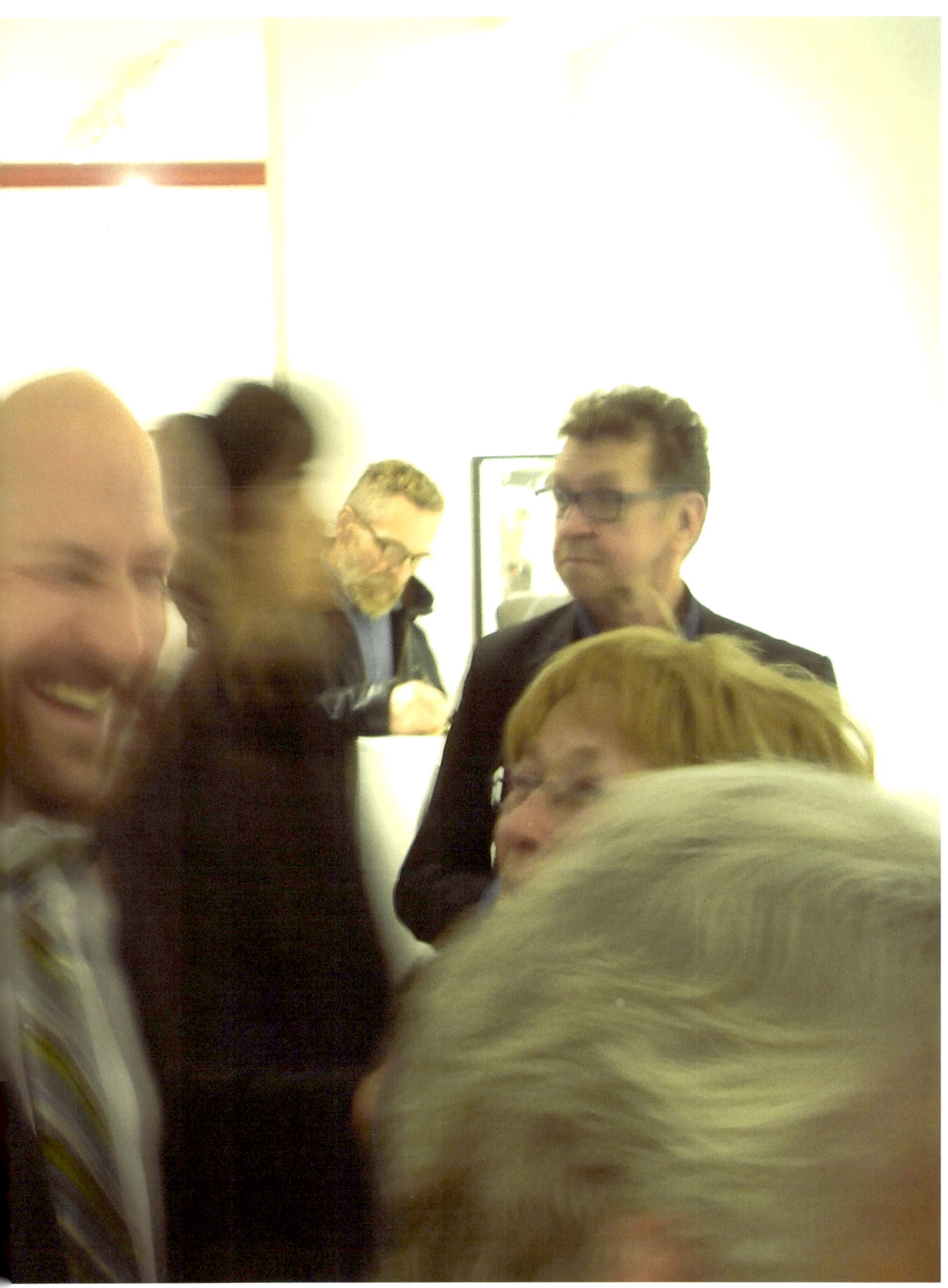

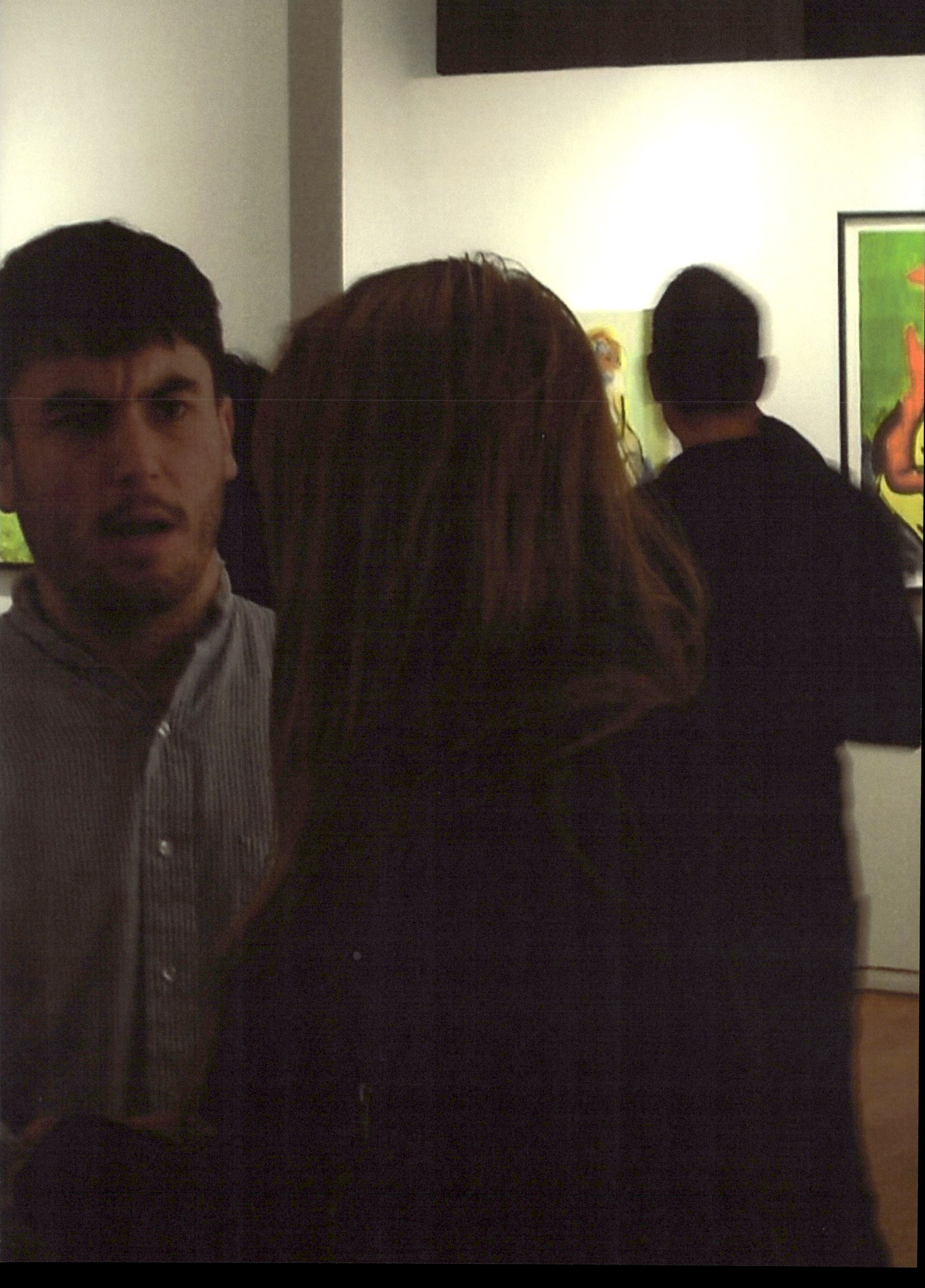

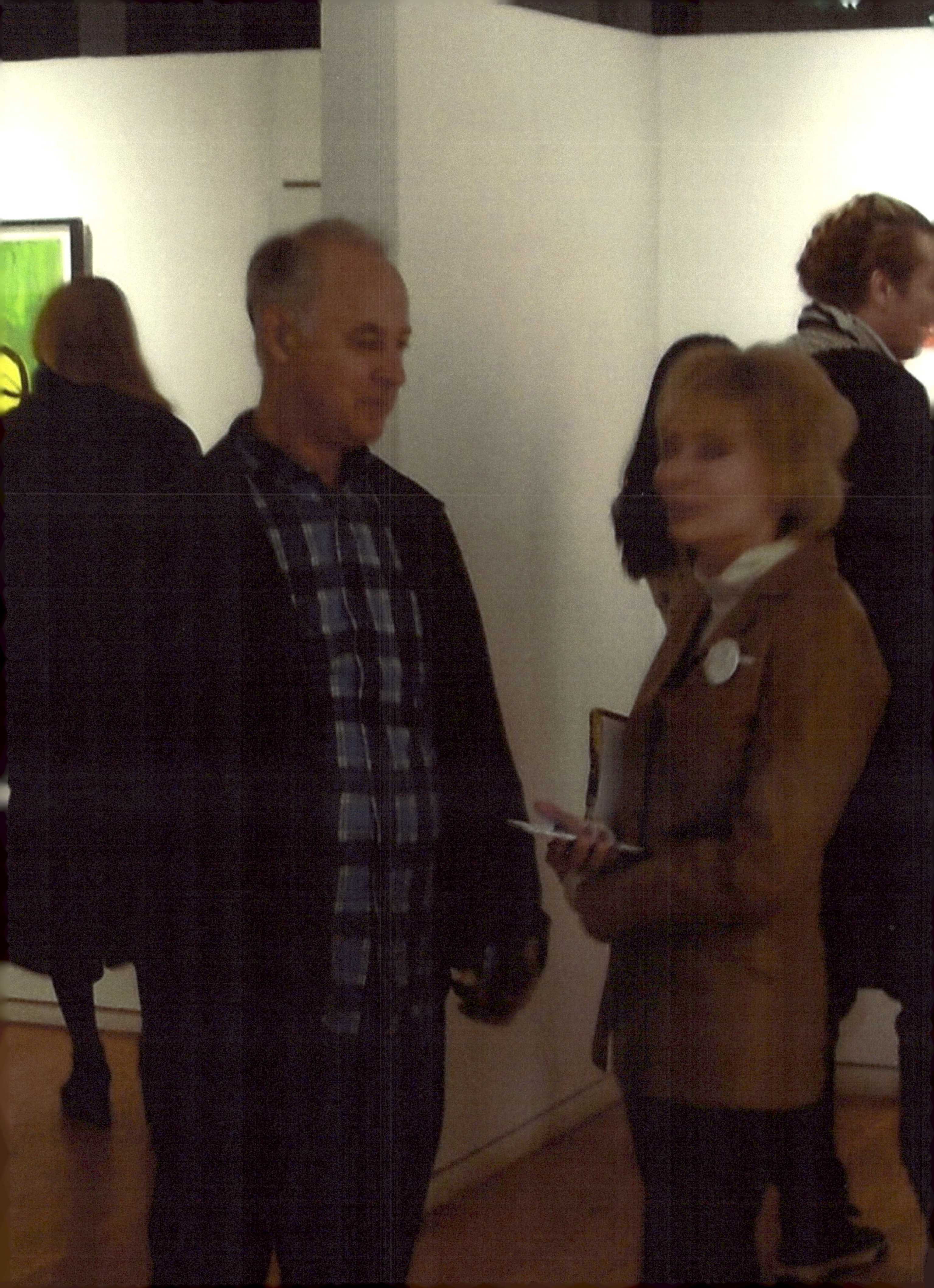

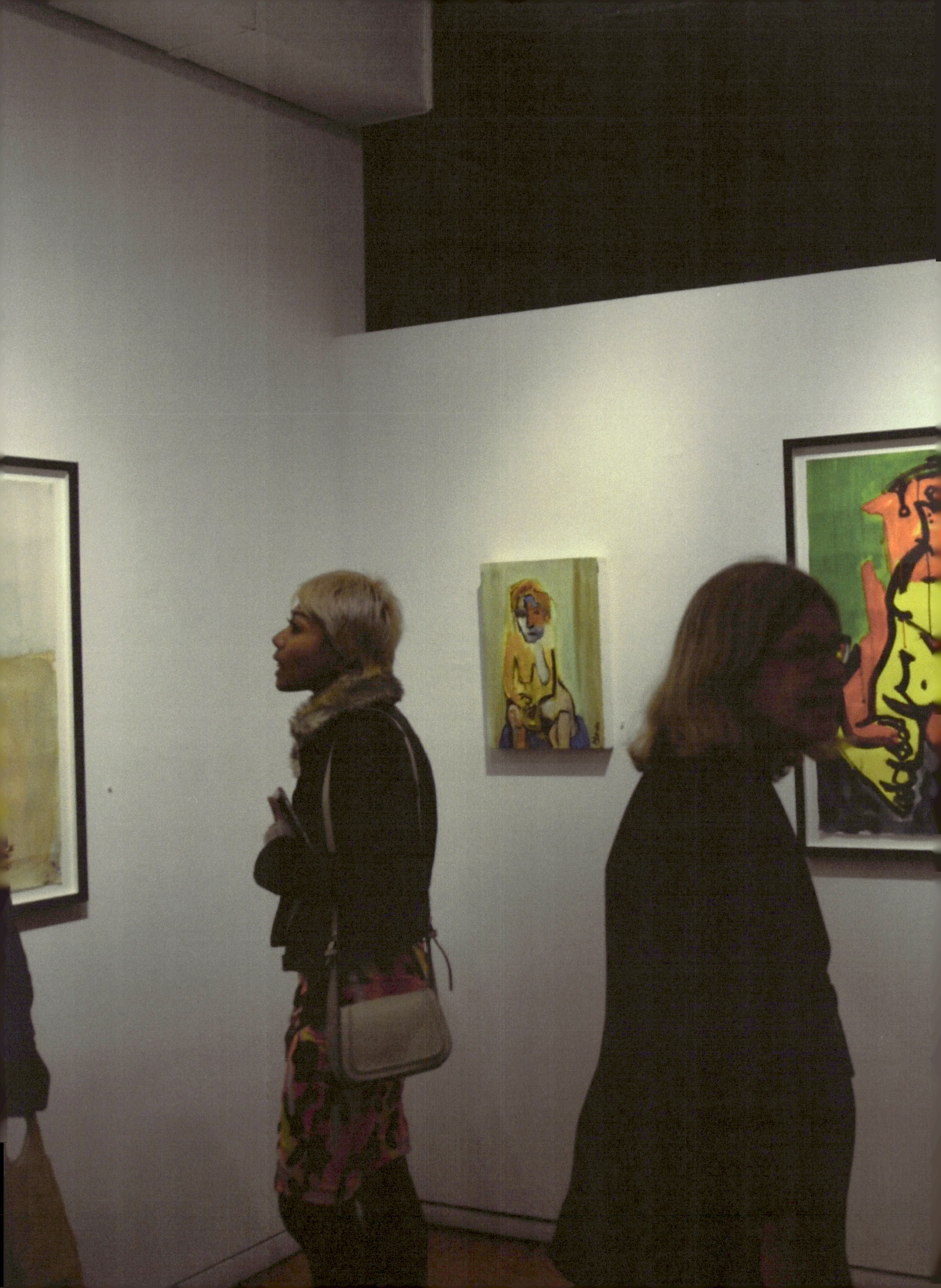

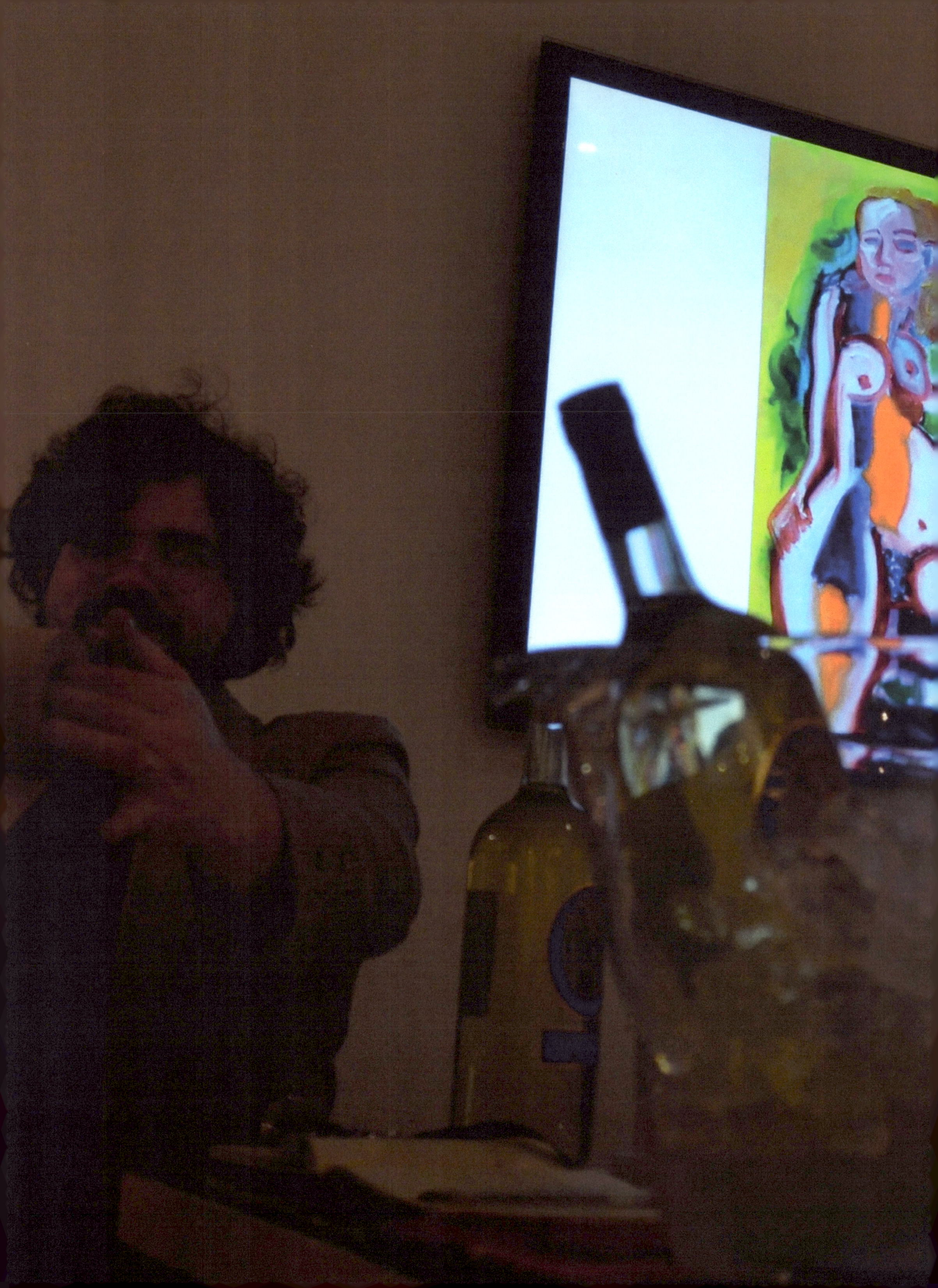

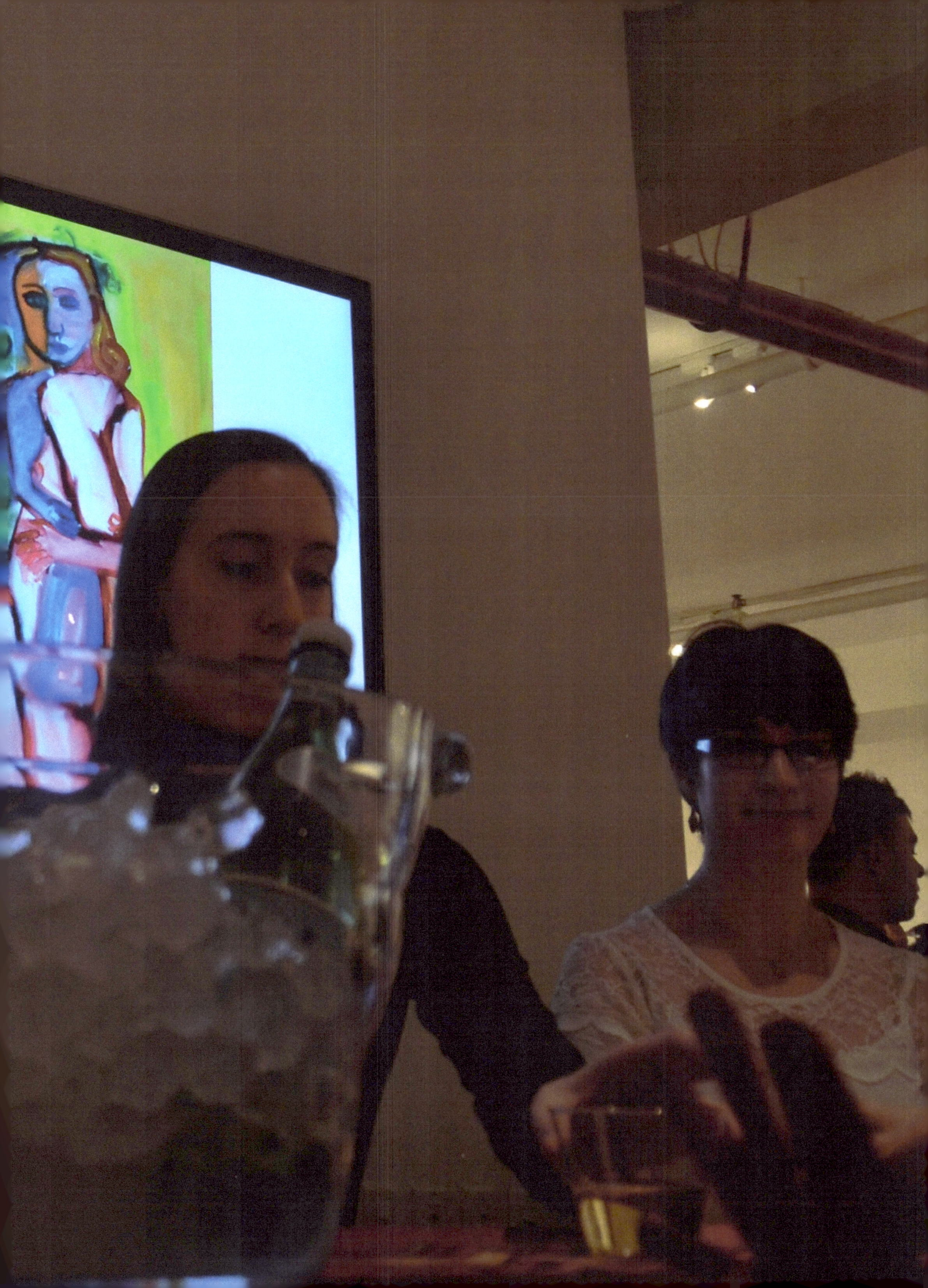

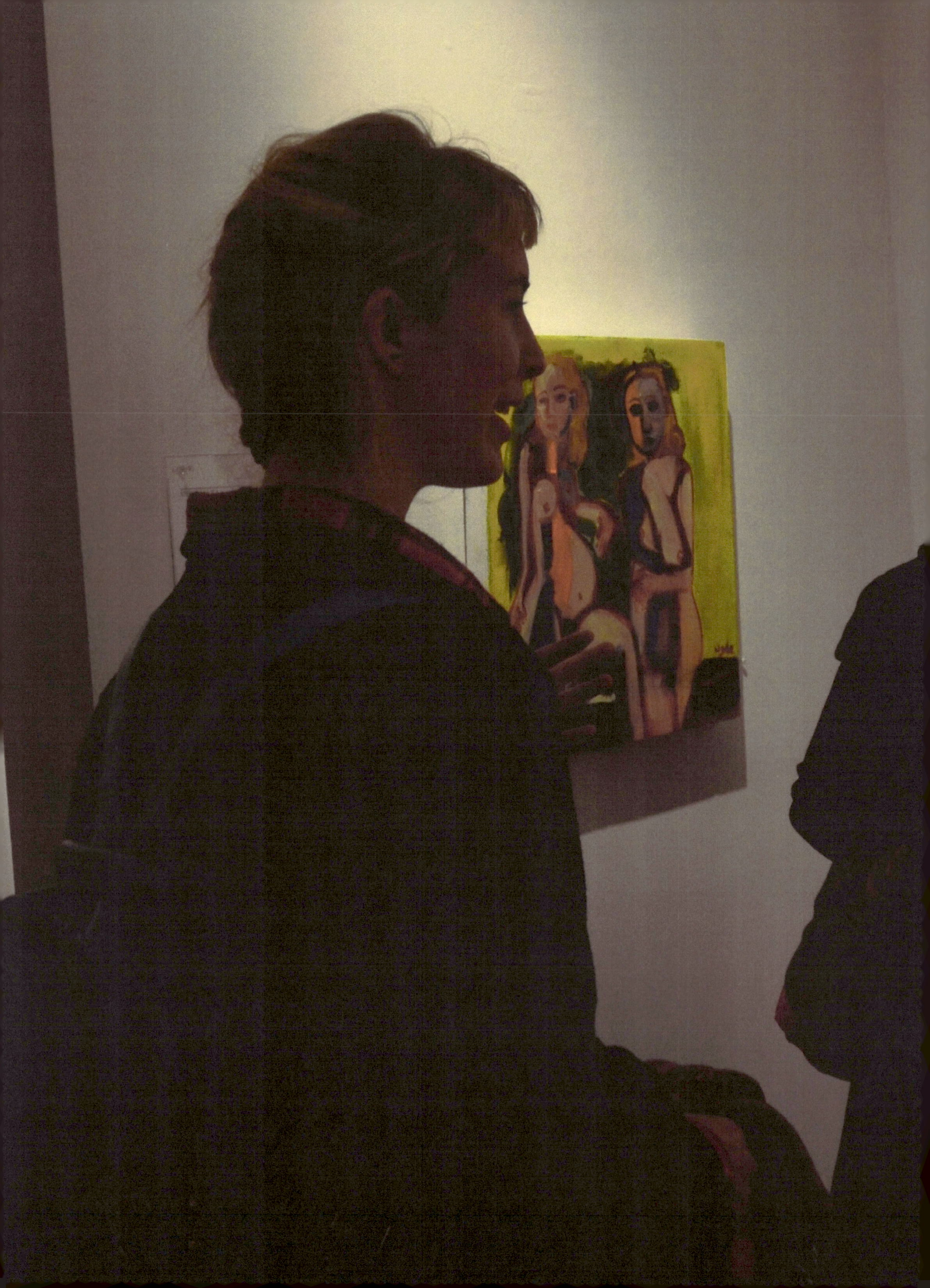

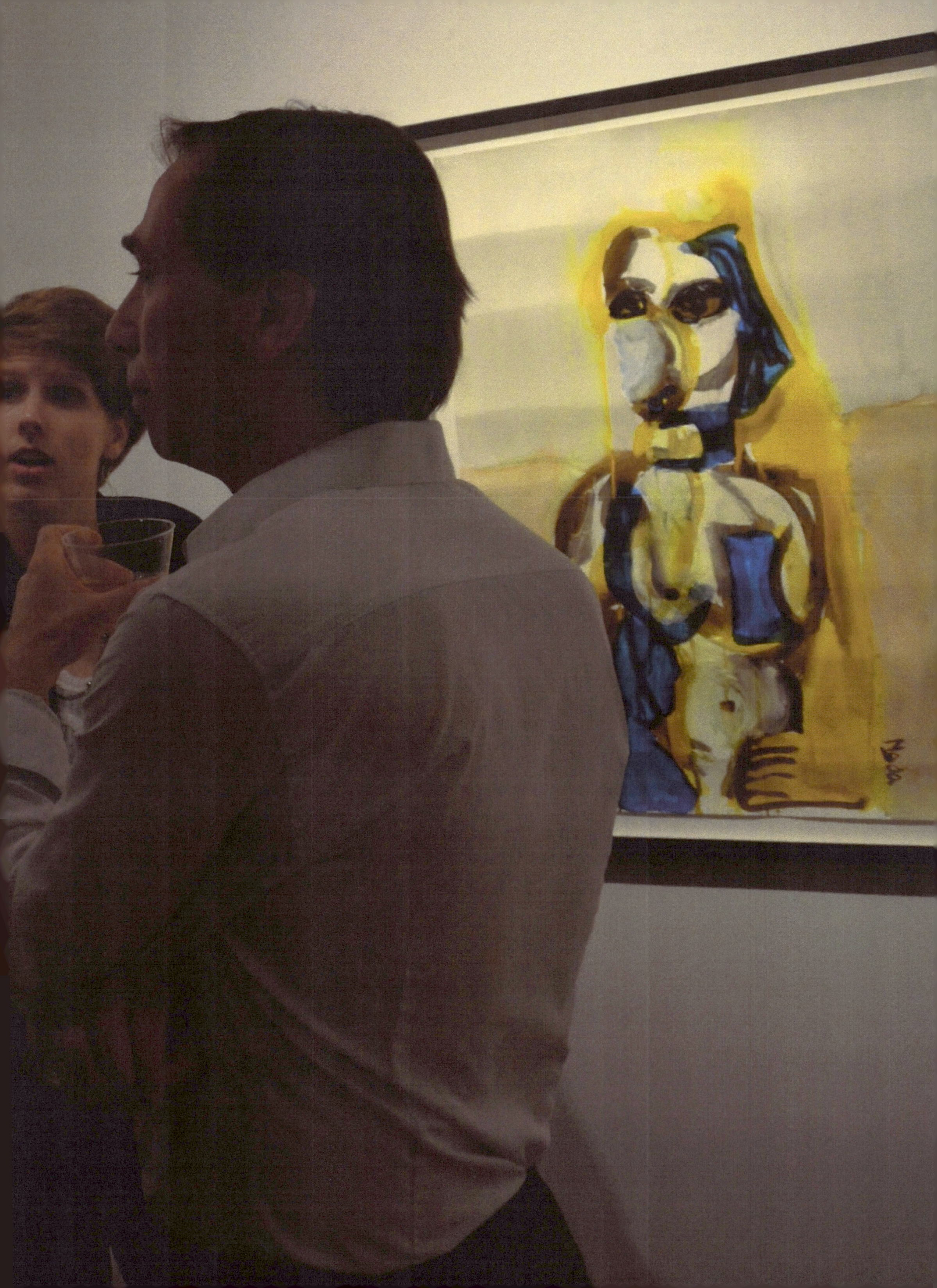

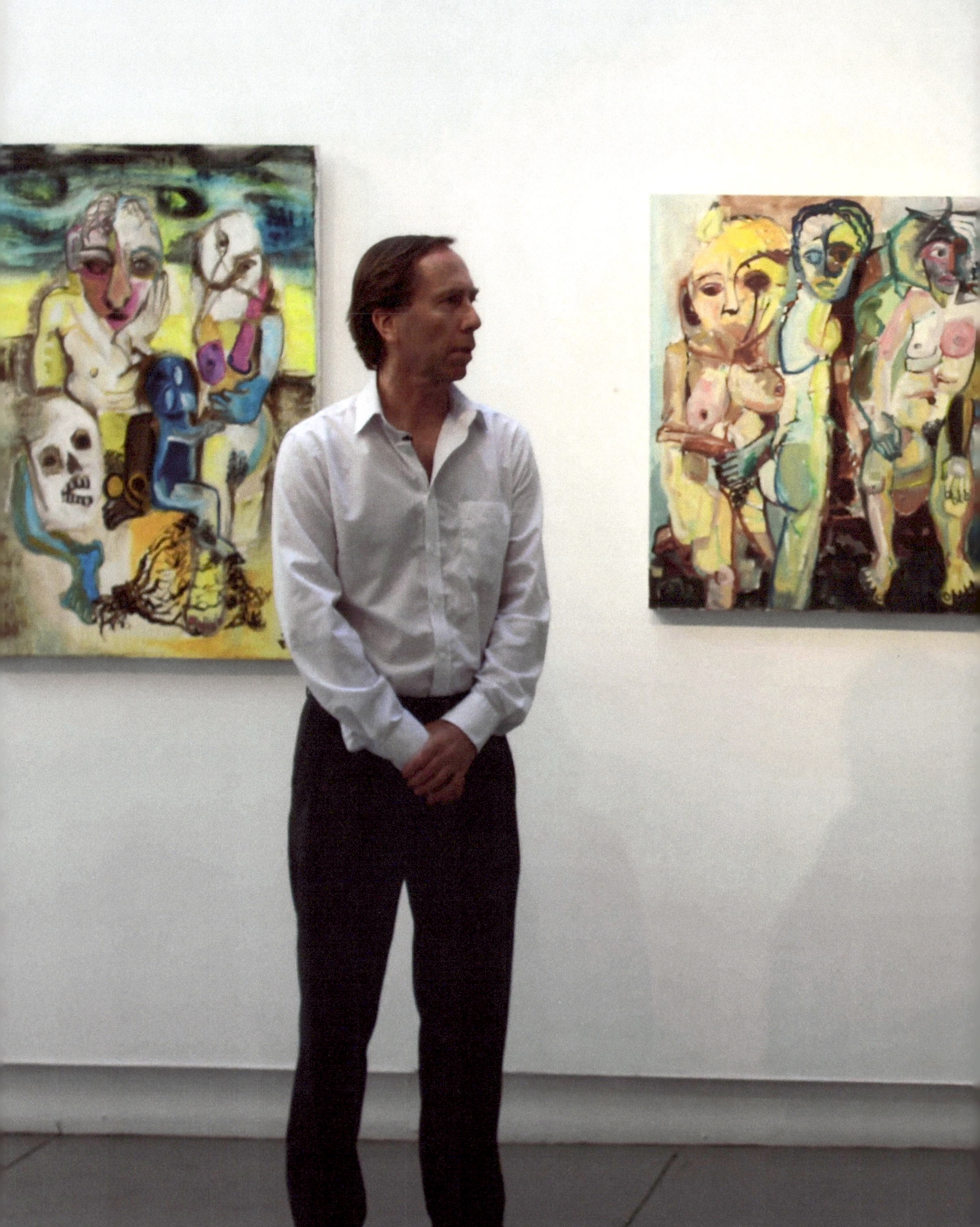

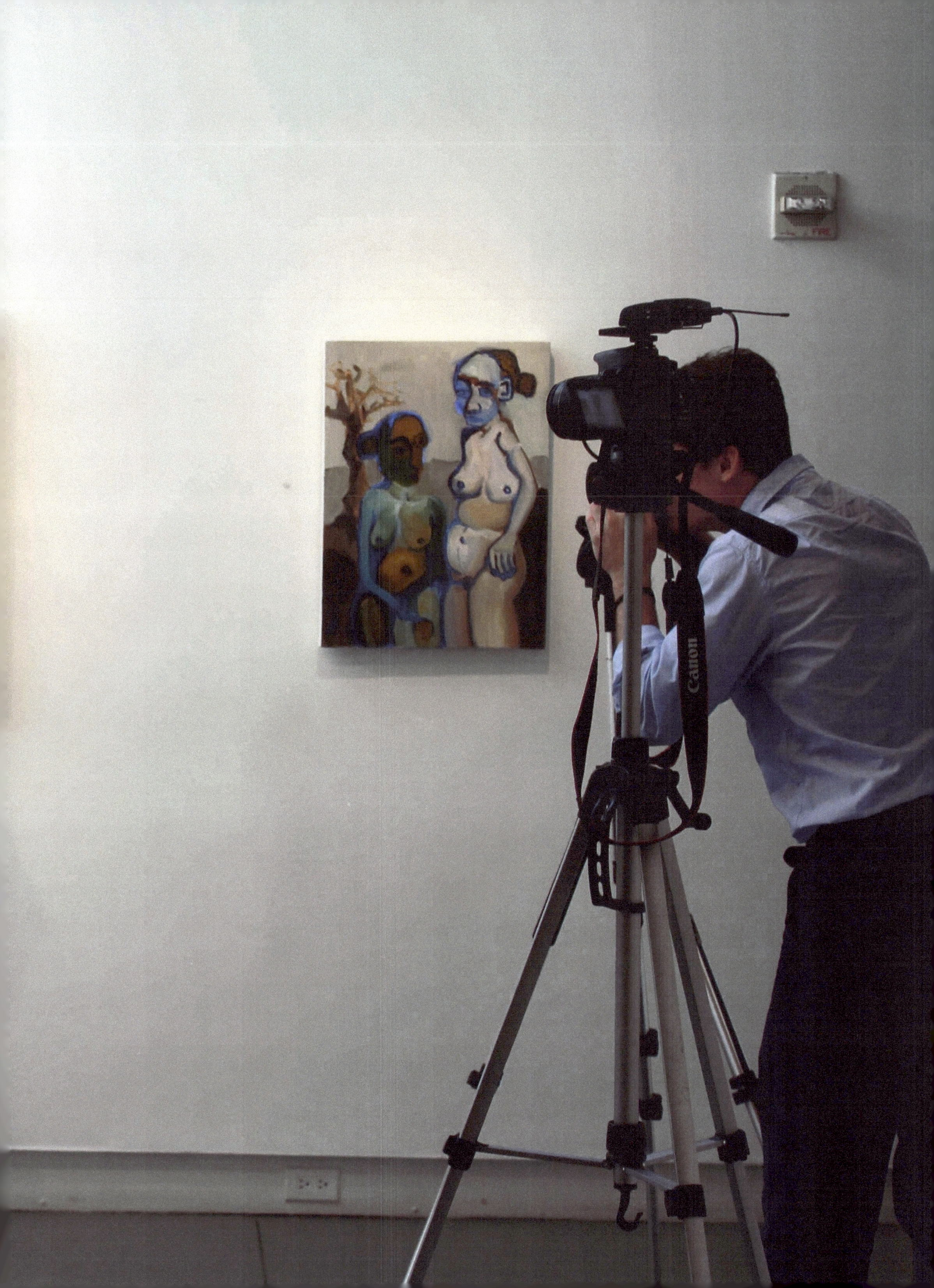

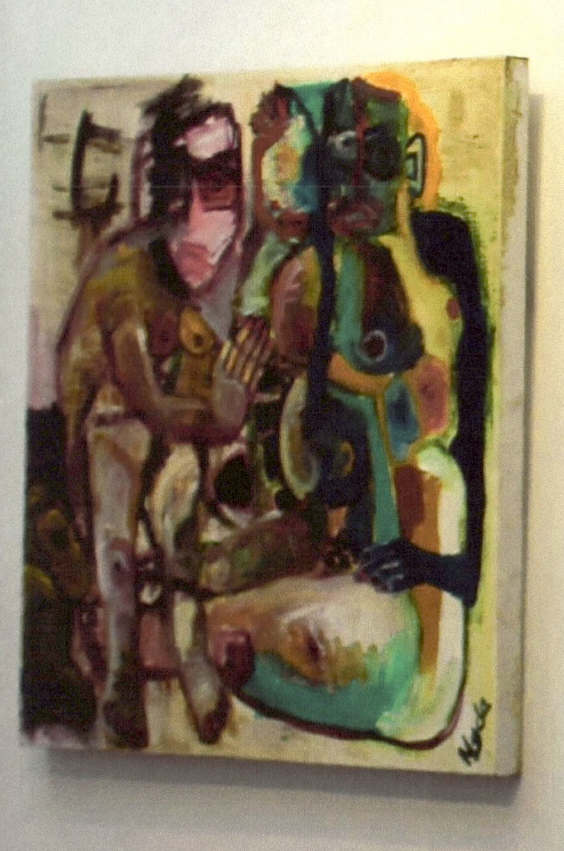

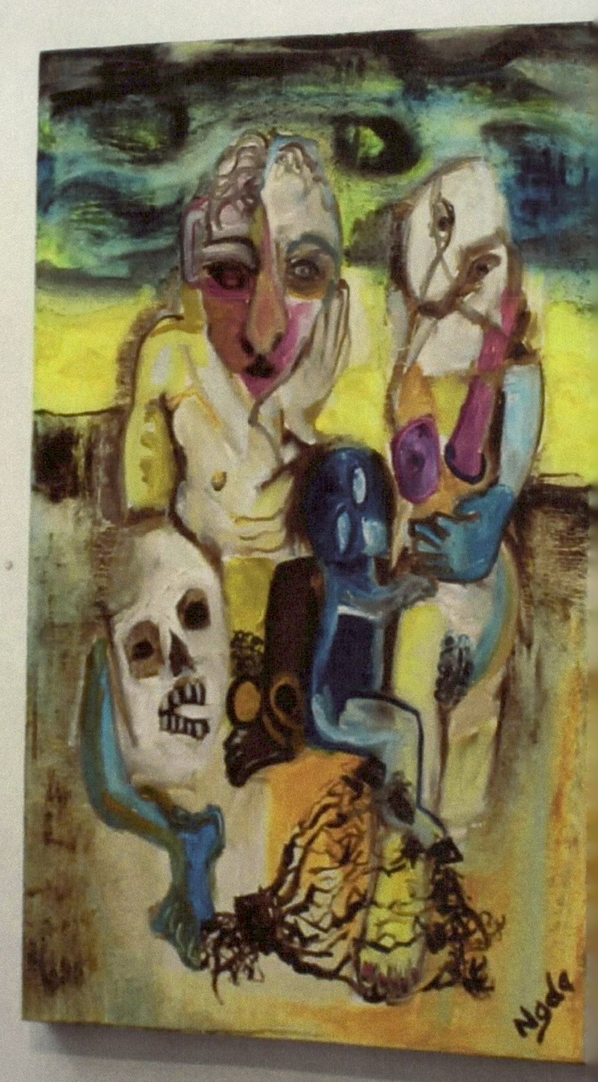

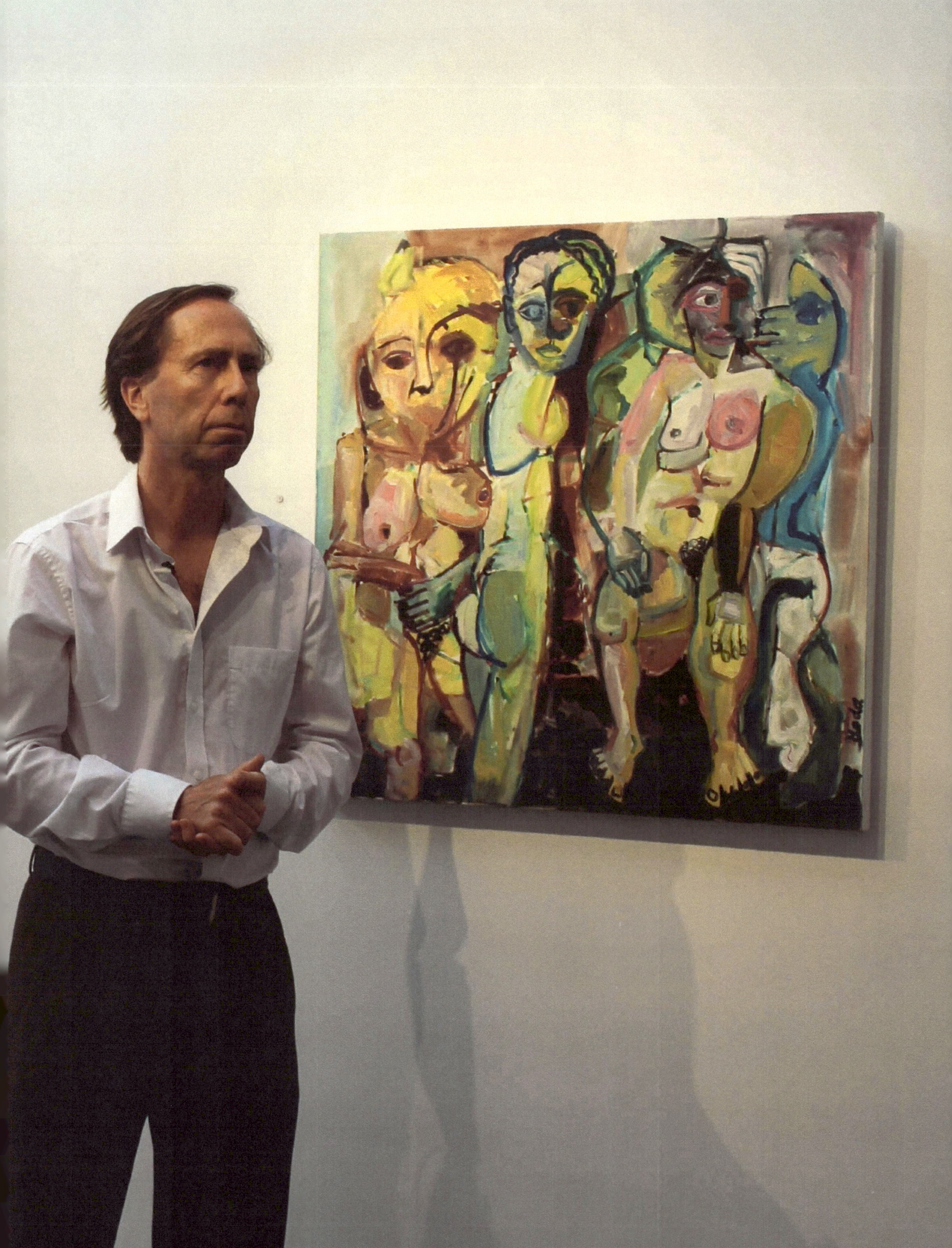

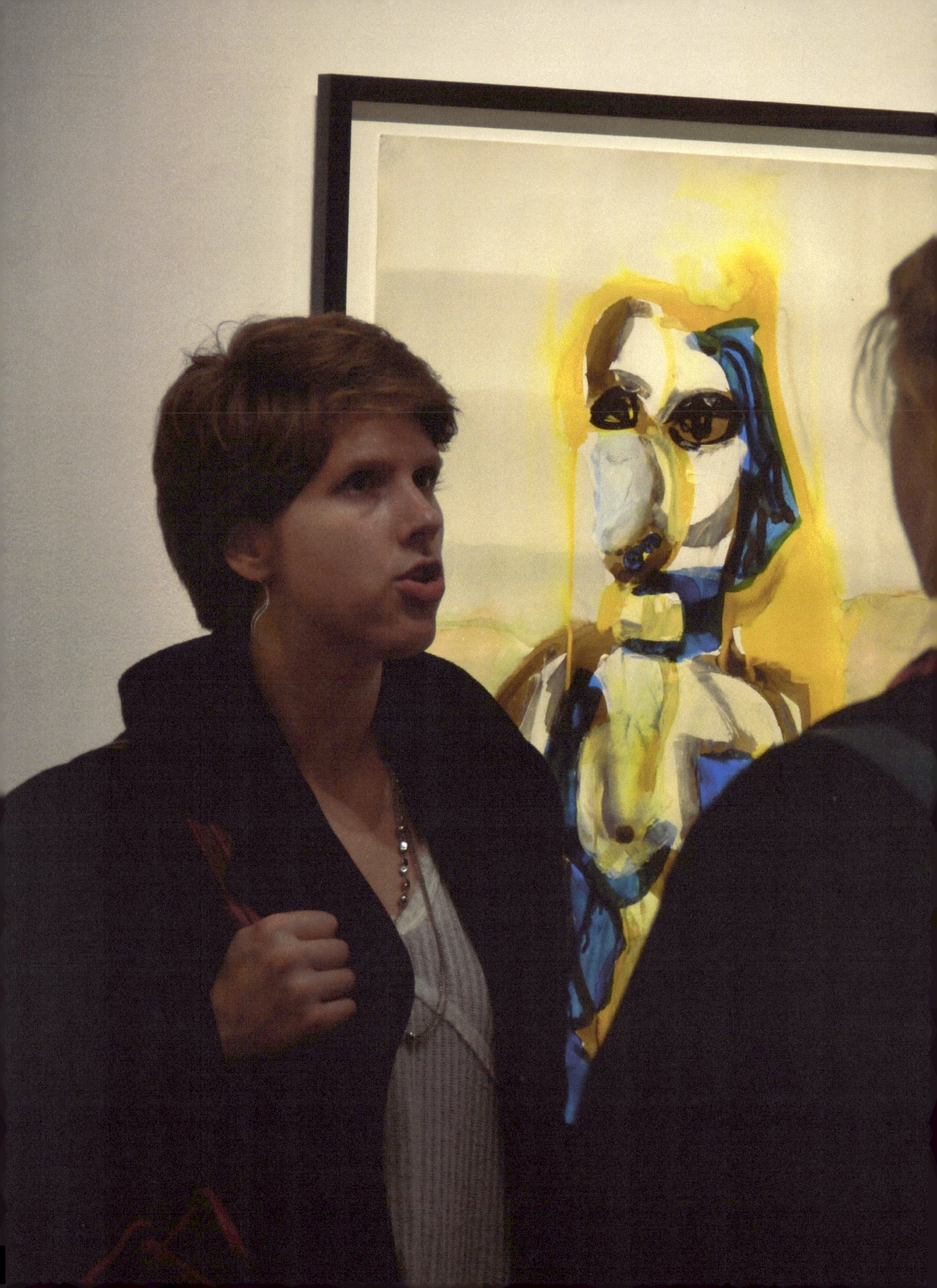

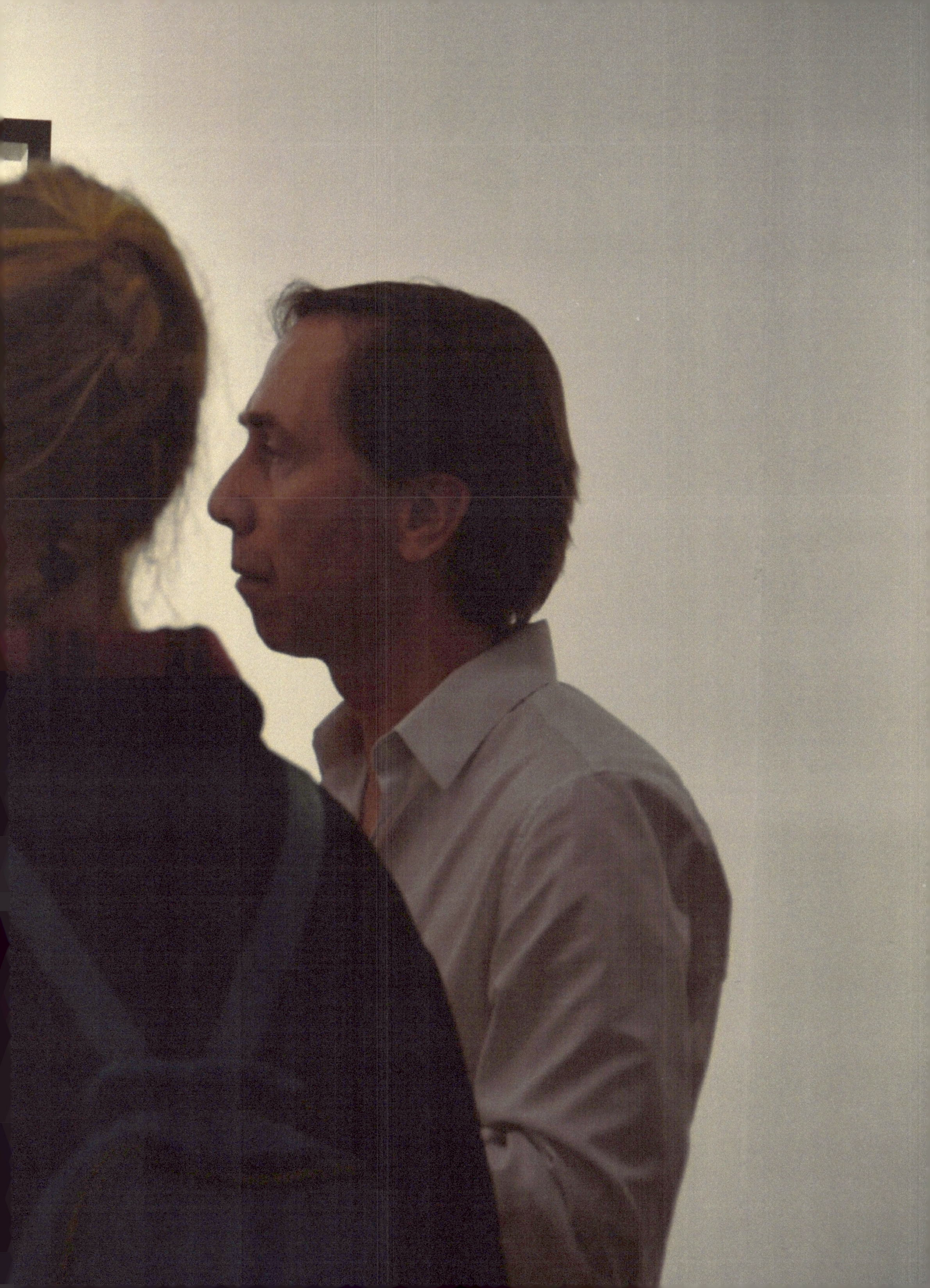

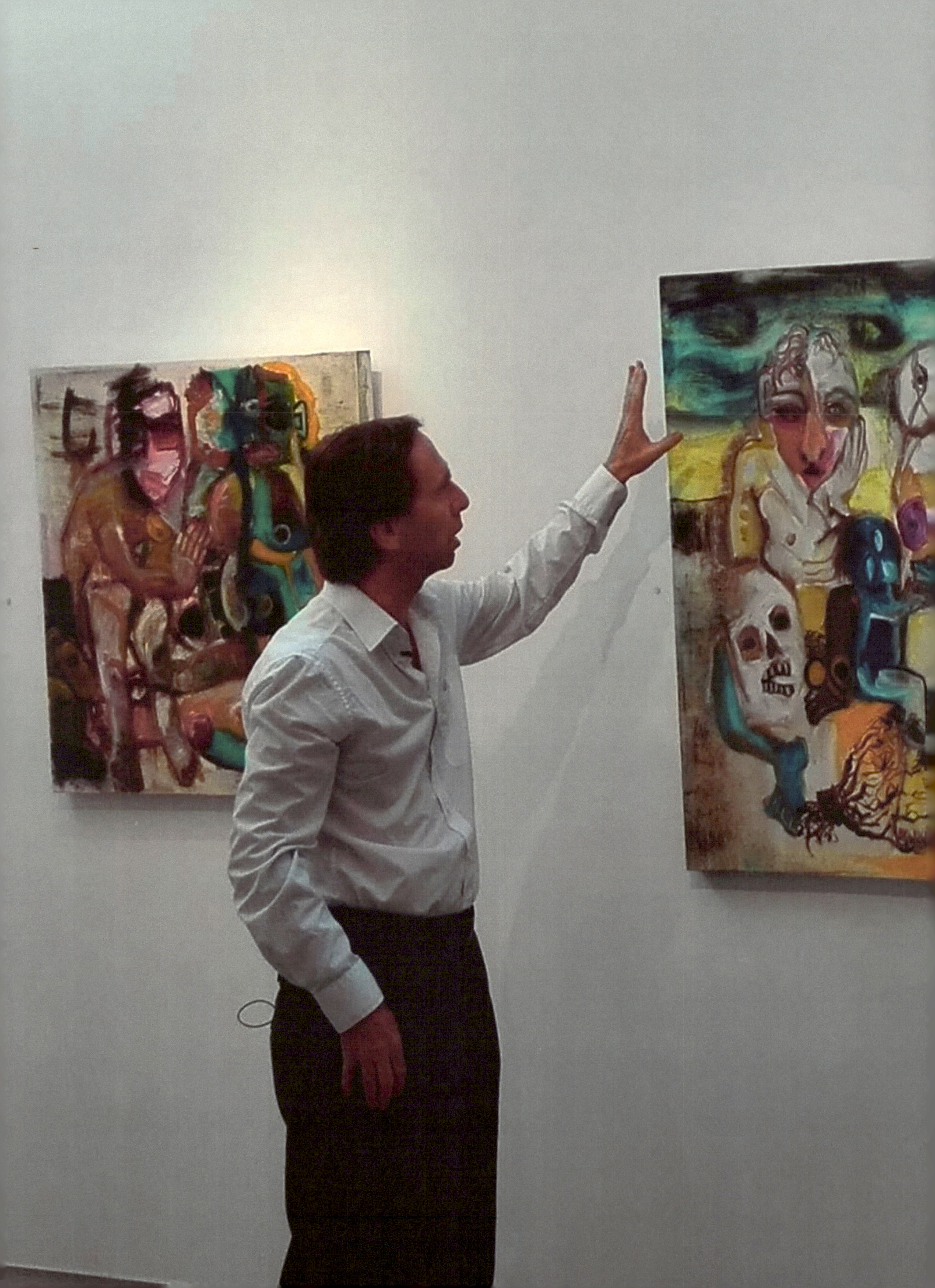

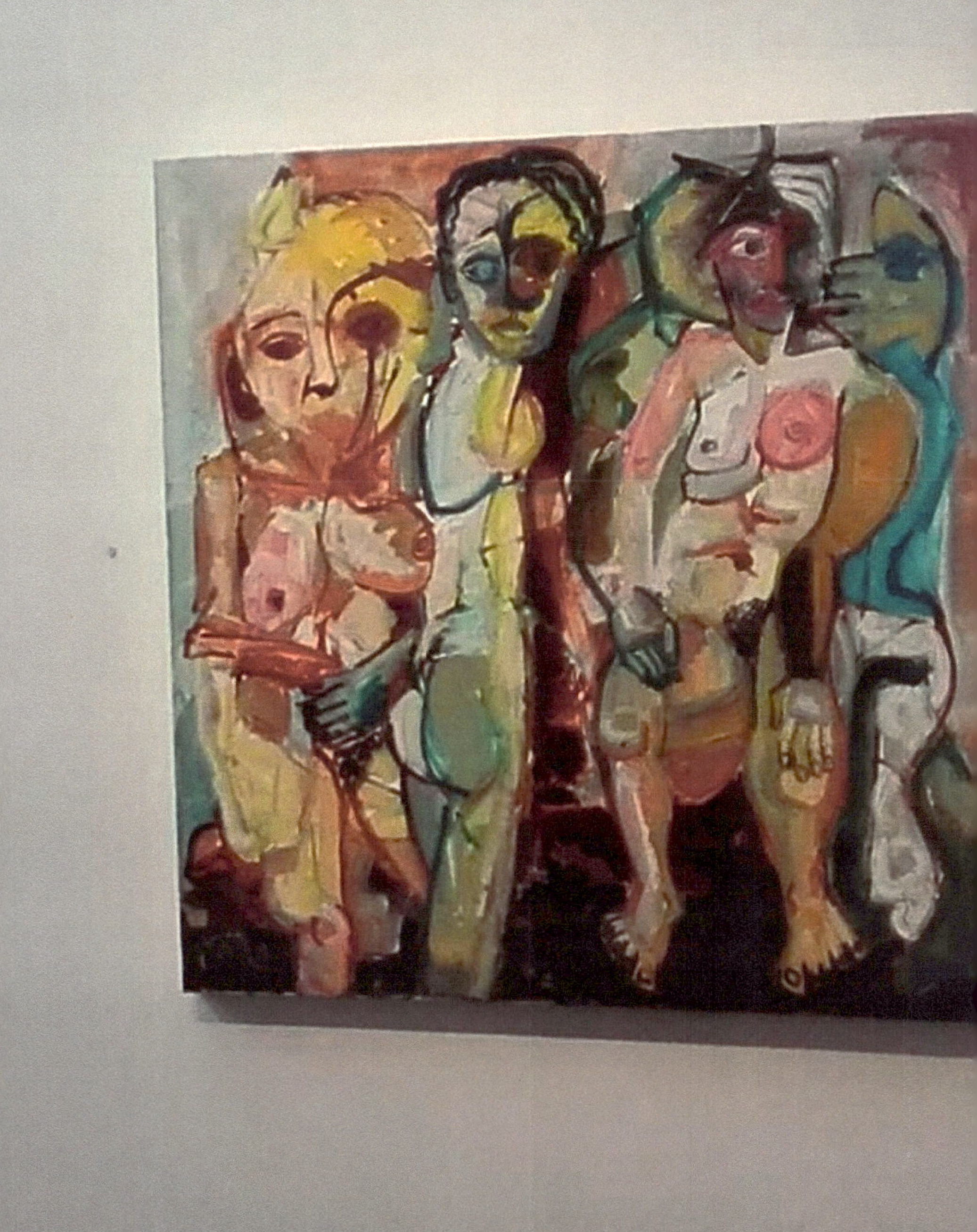

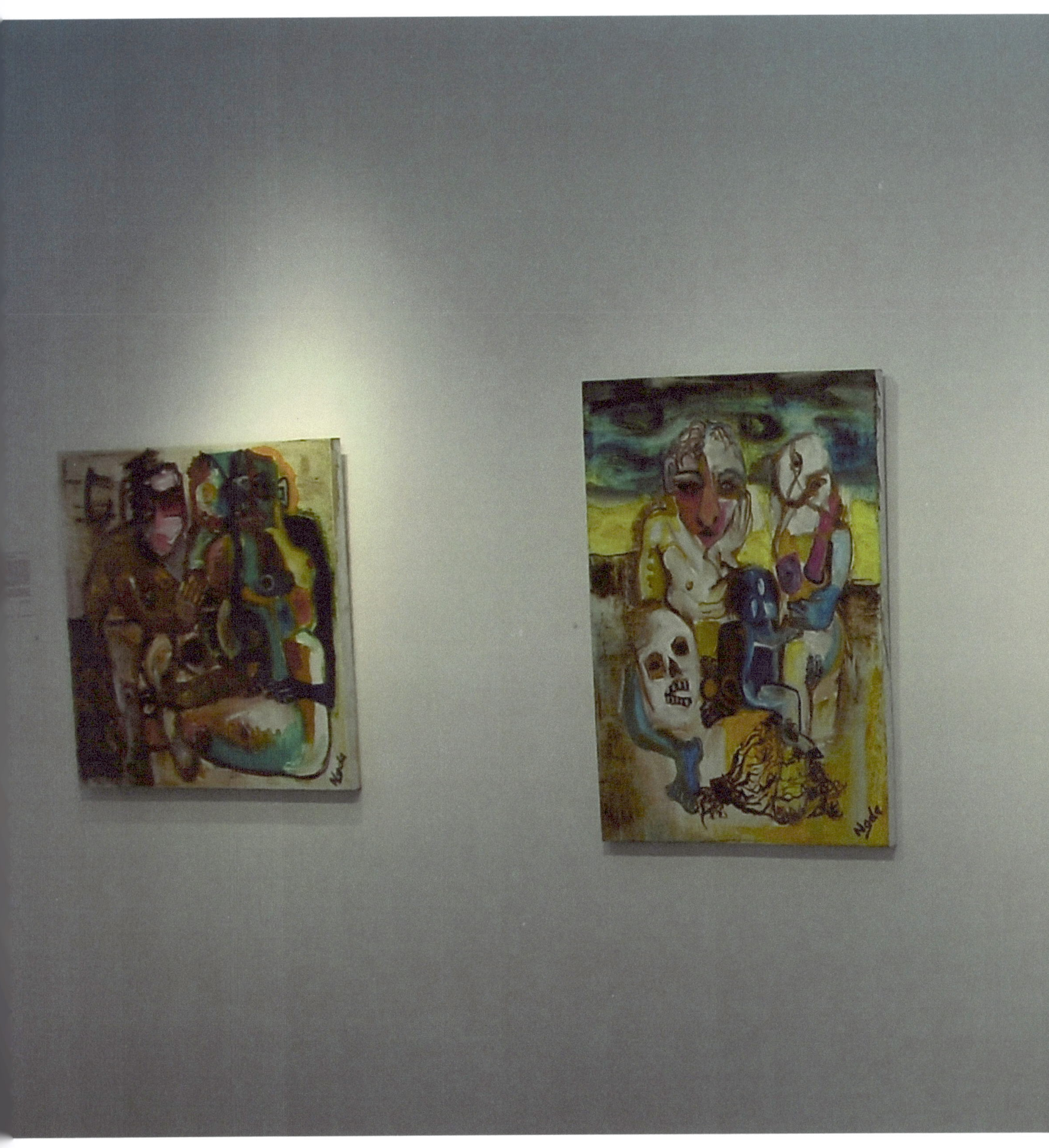

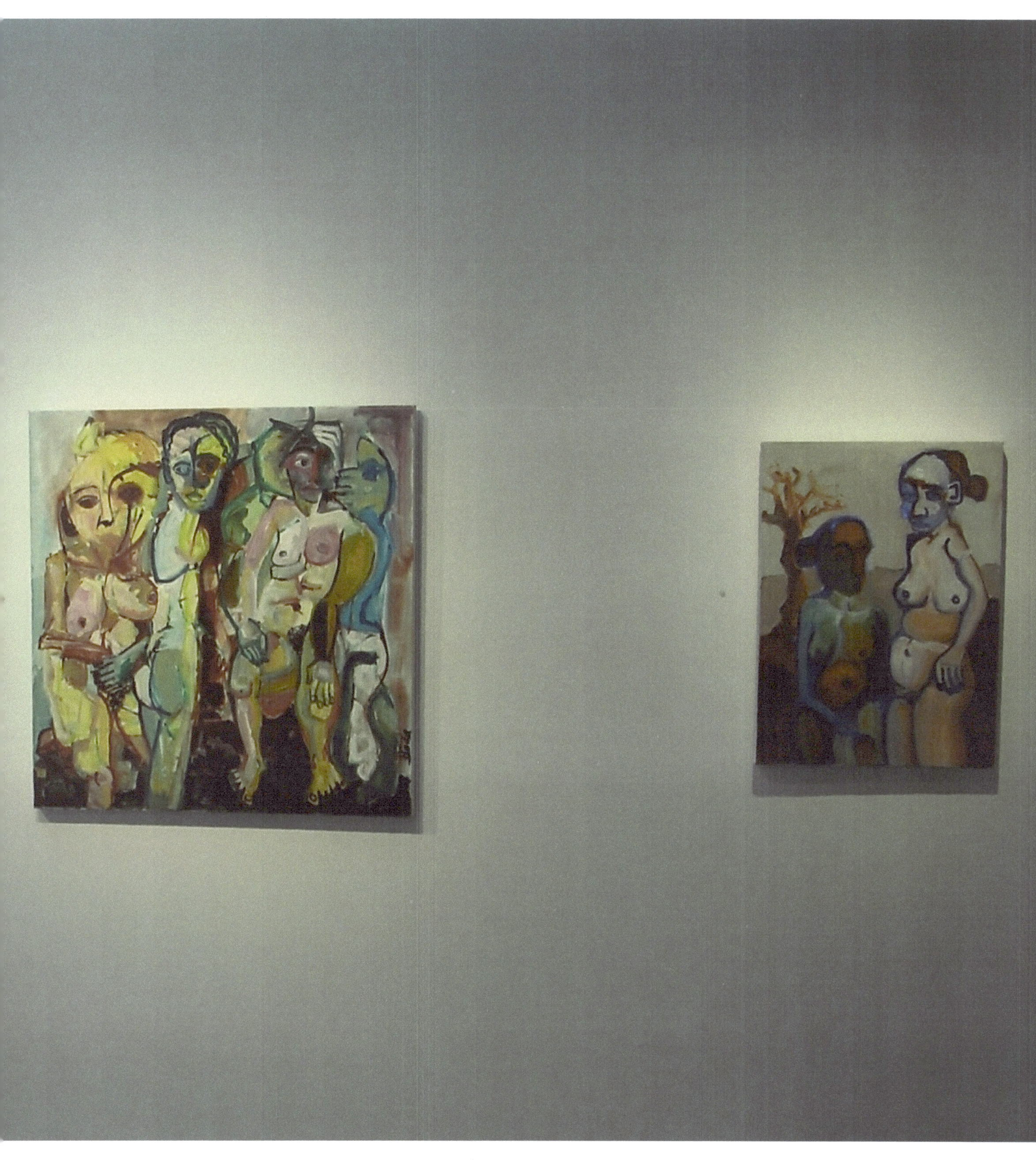

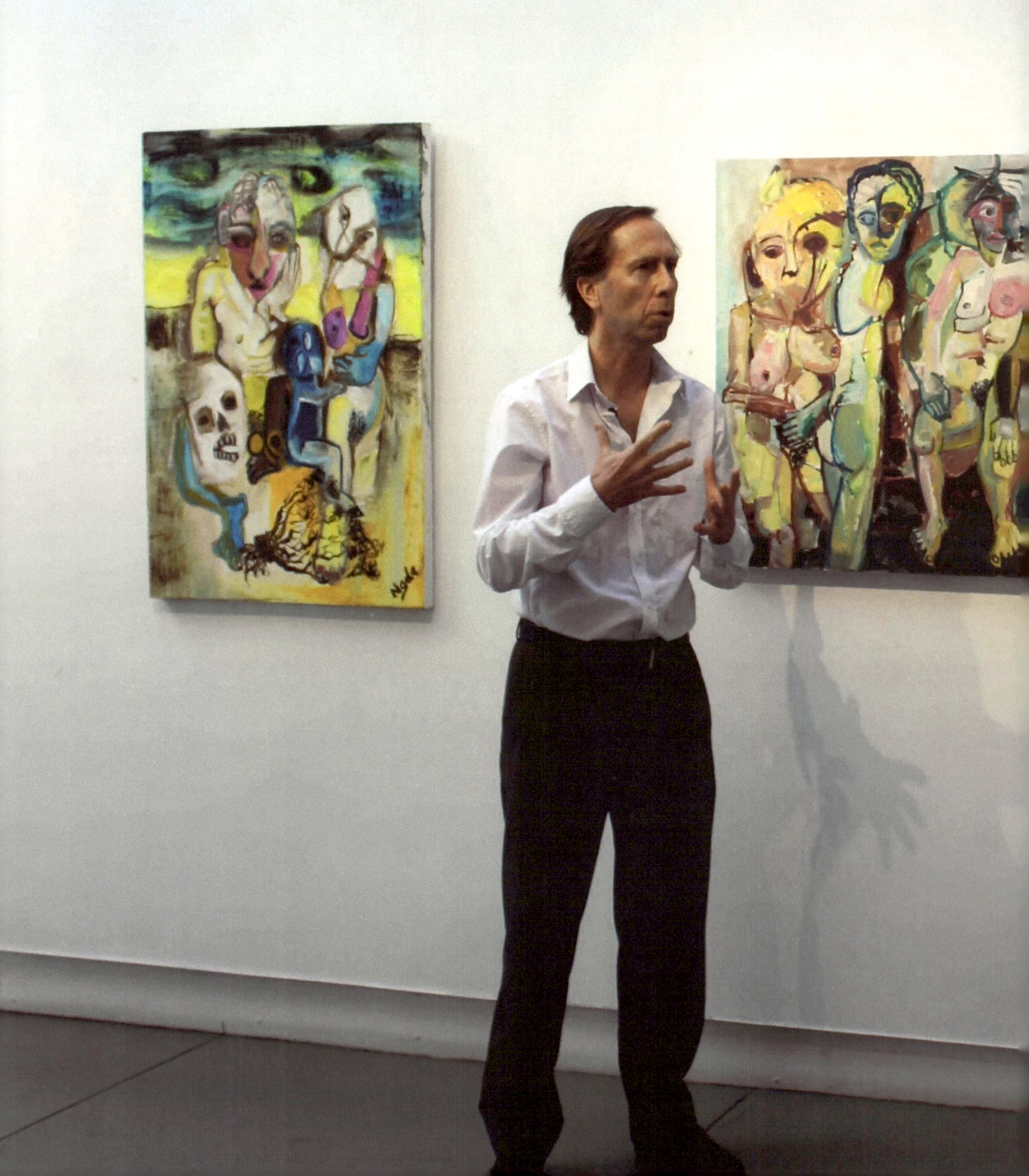

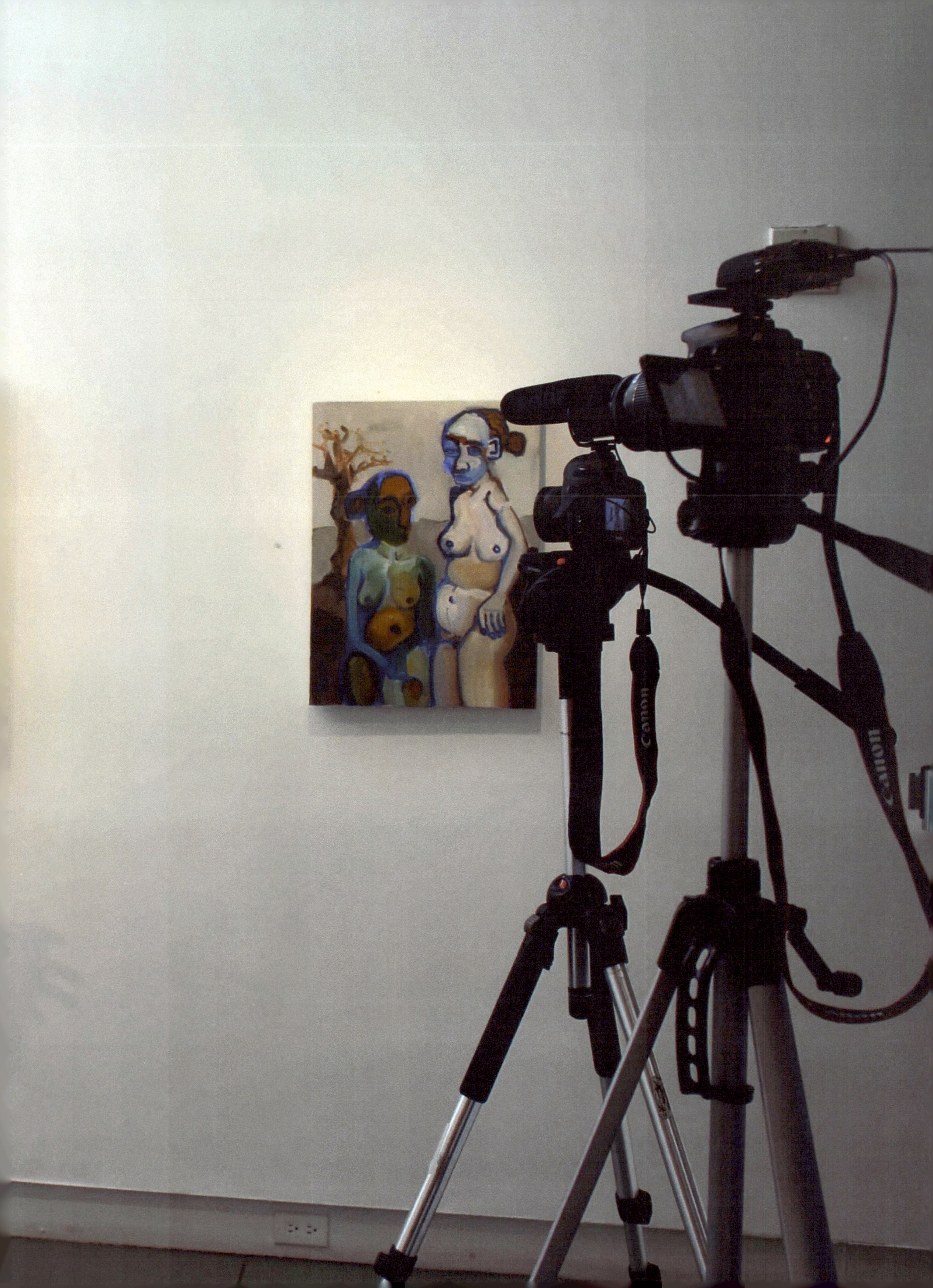

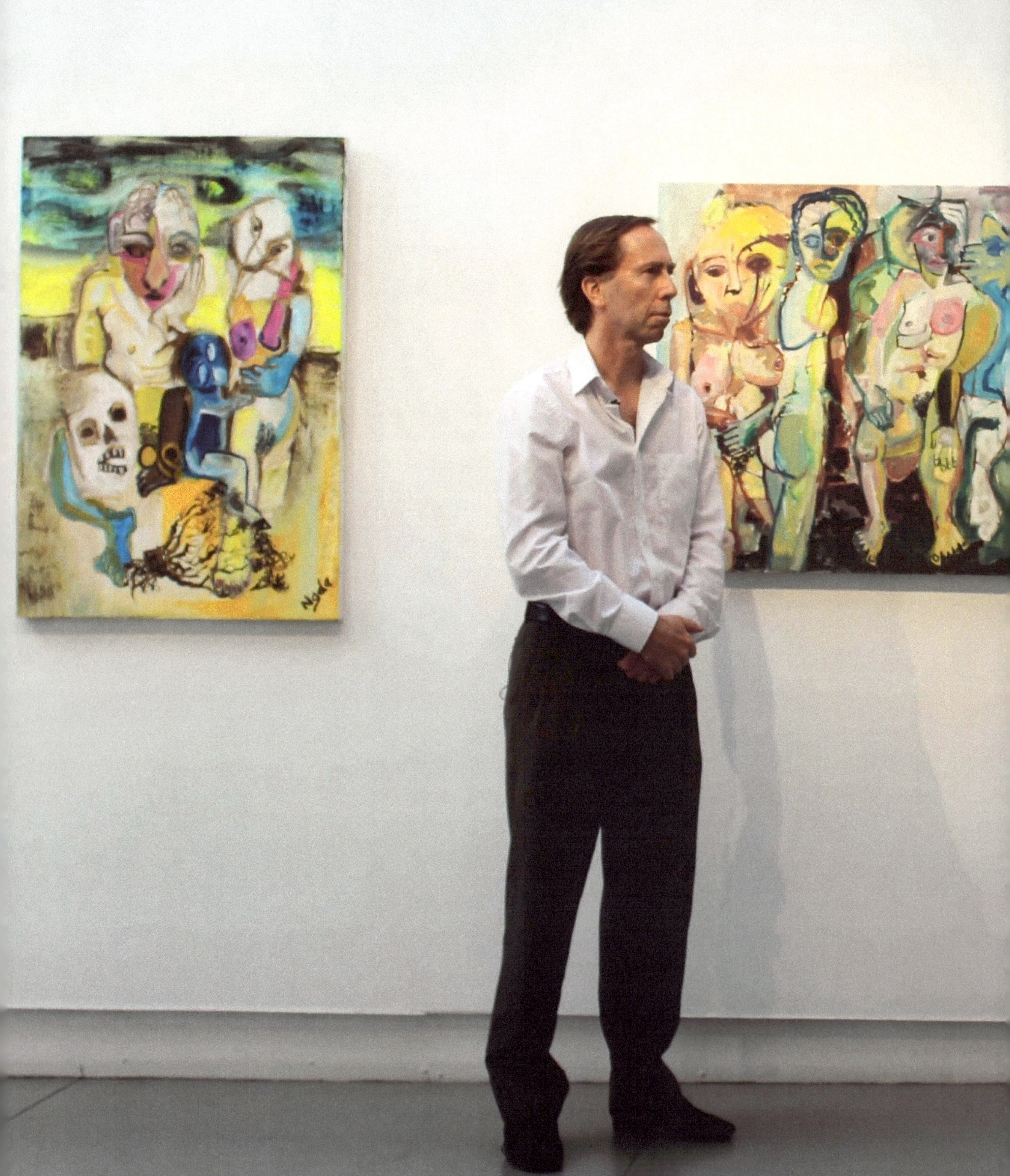

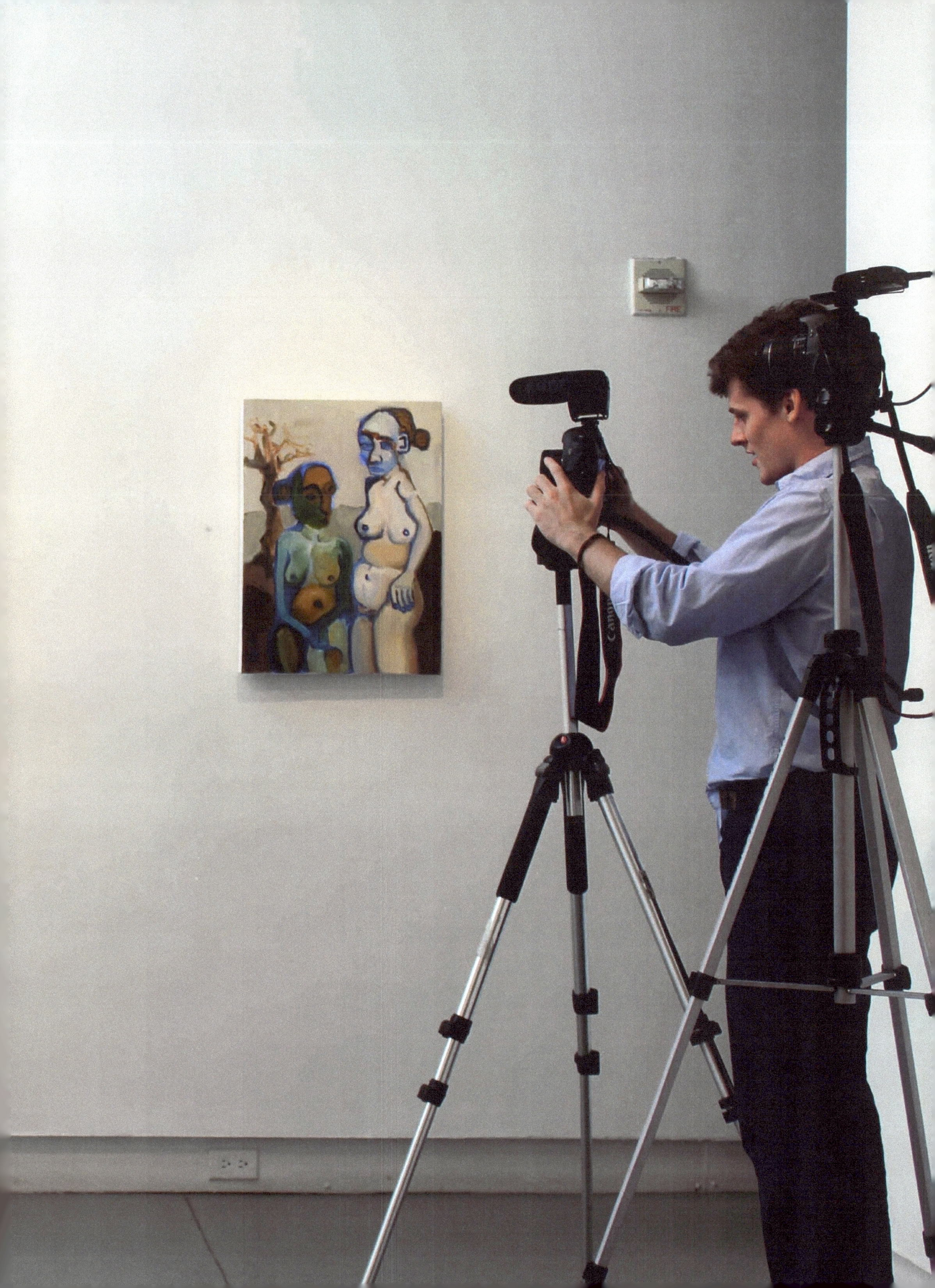

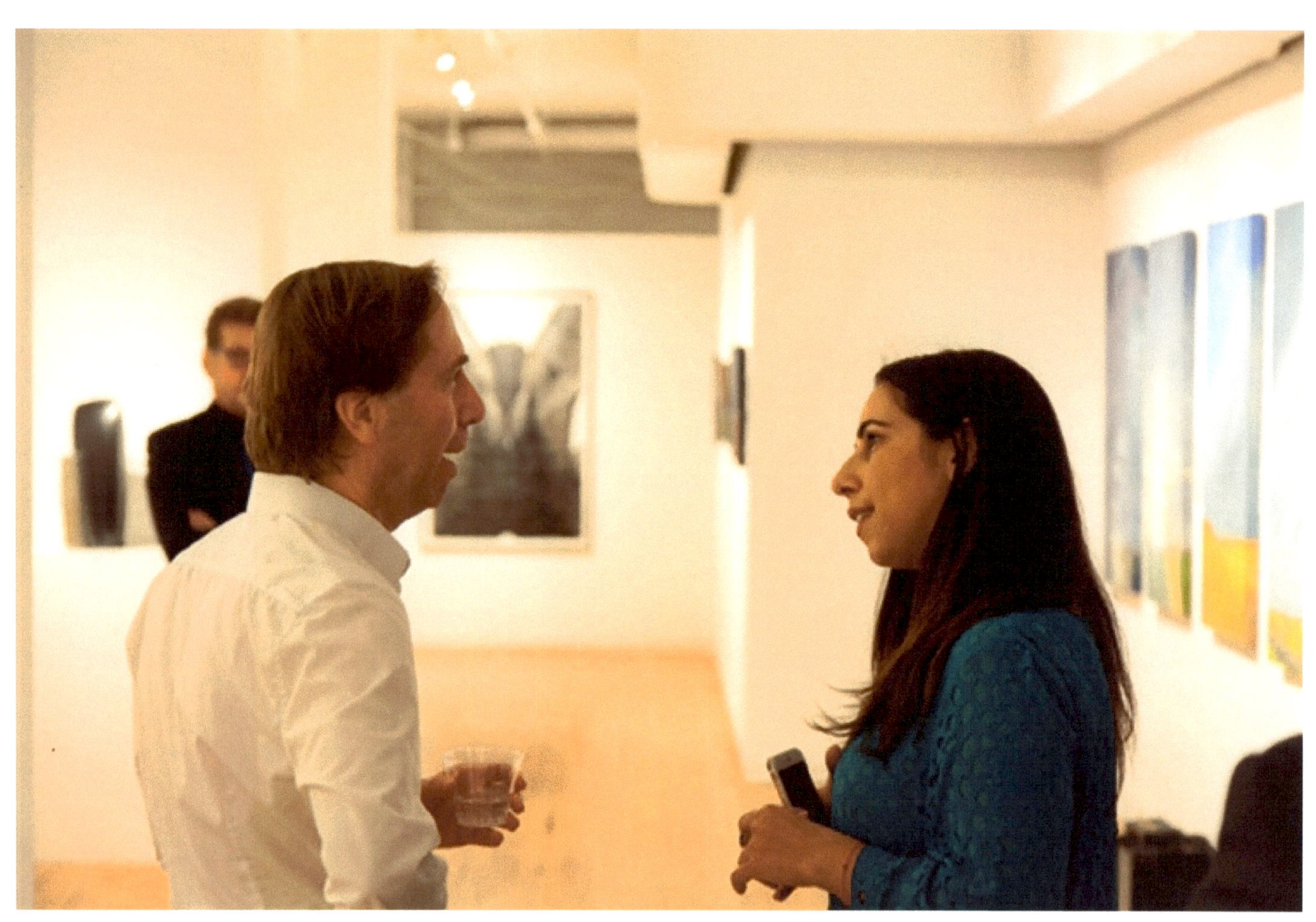

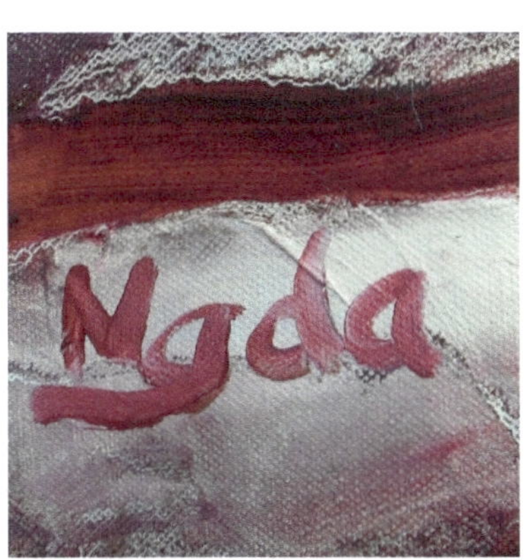

OTHER WORKS

“SELF PORTRAIT”

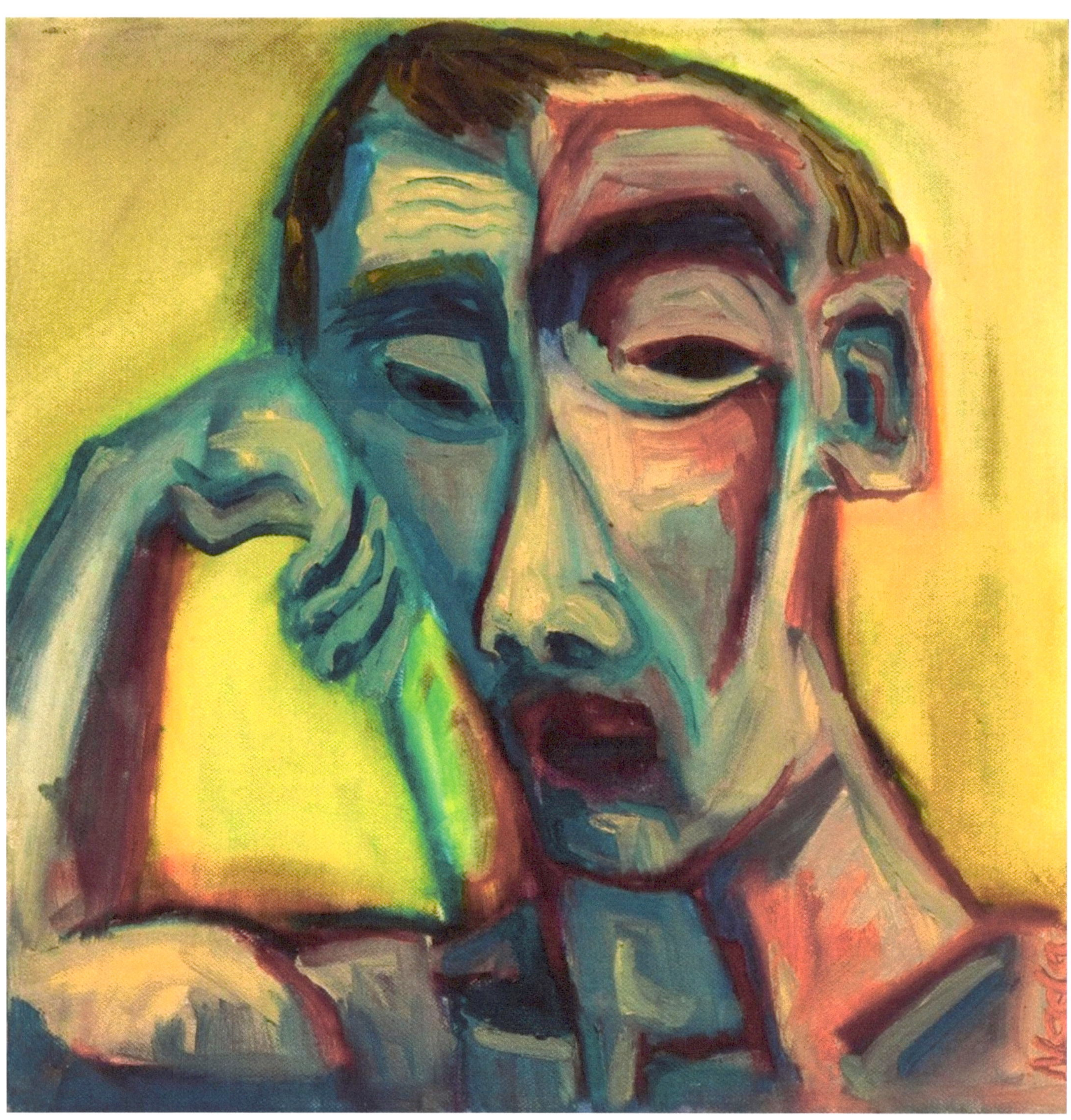

Technique: Oil painting on canvas
Size: 40 cm x 50 cm
Year: 2014

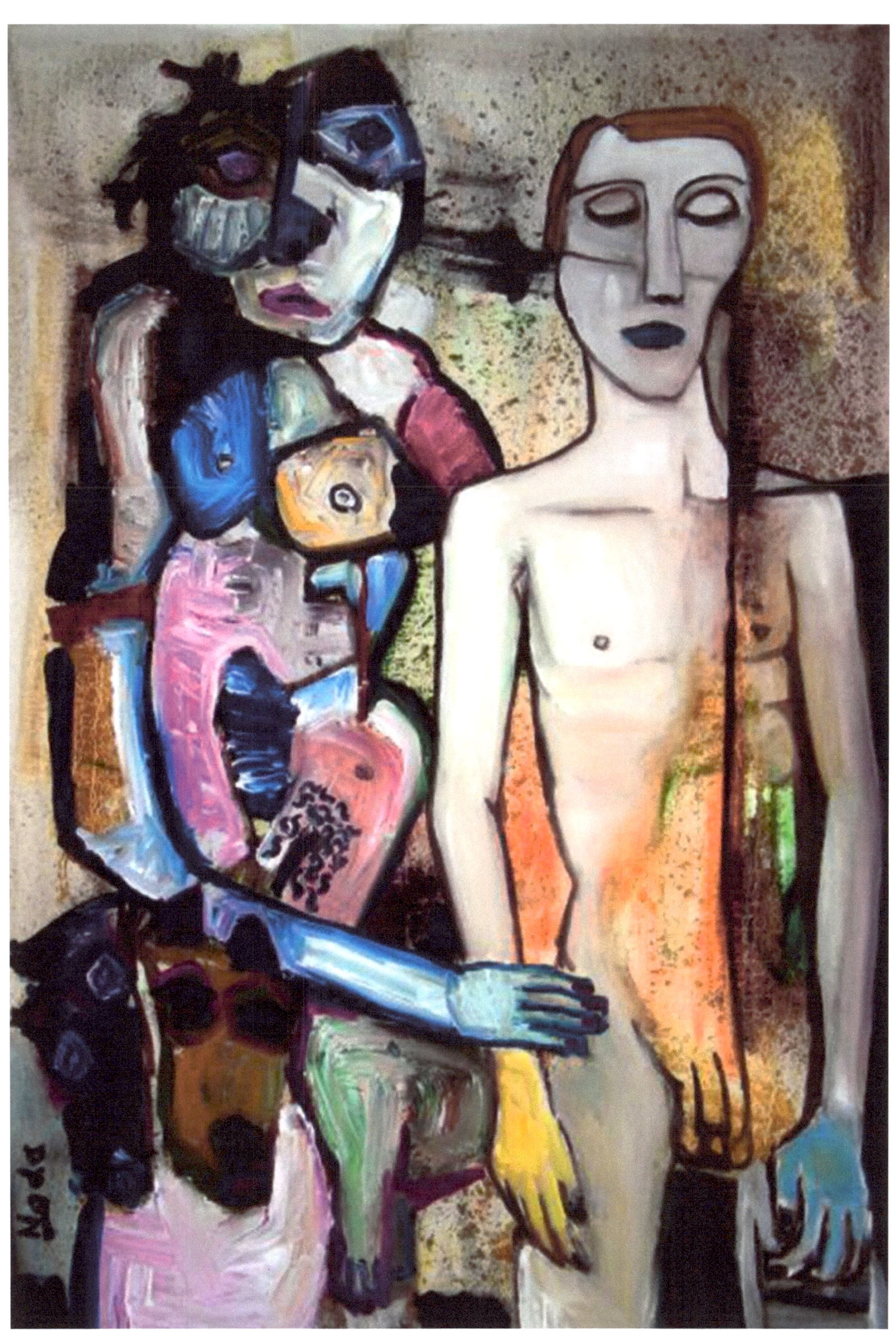

"DESERT MOON AND WIND"

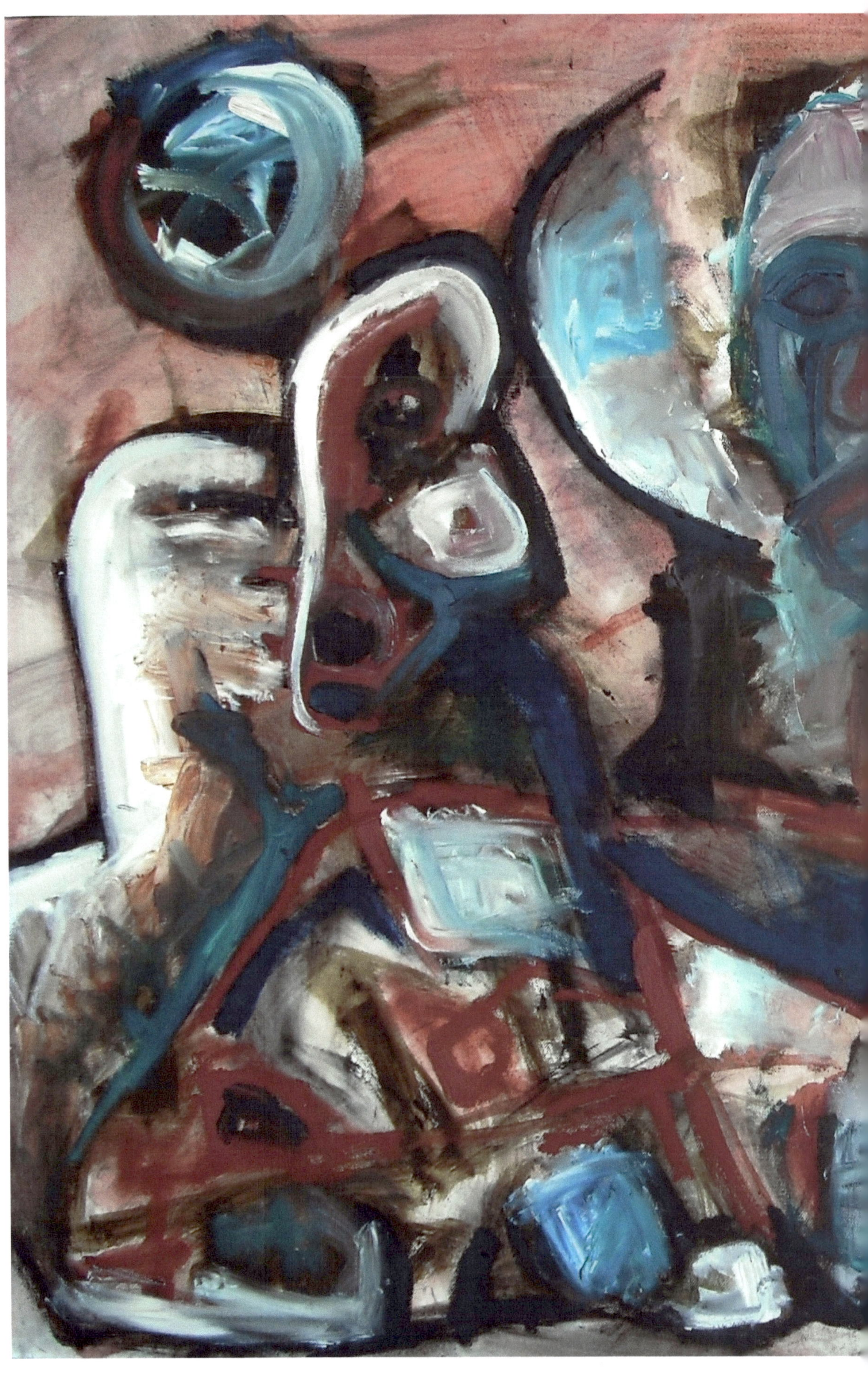

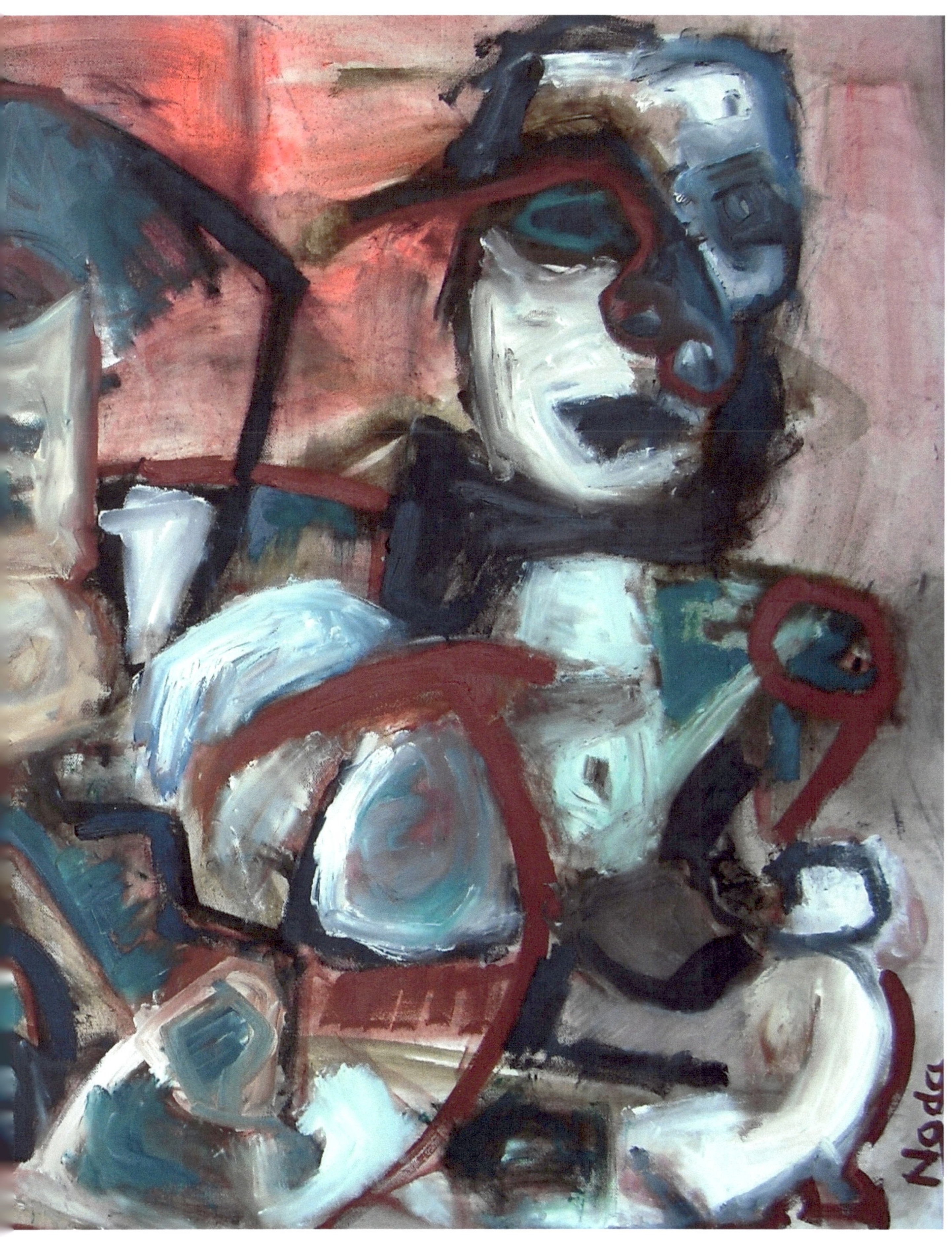

Noda

"NUBIAN GIRL WITH HORSE"

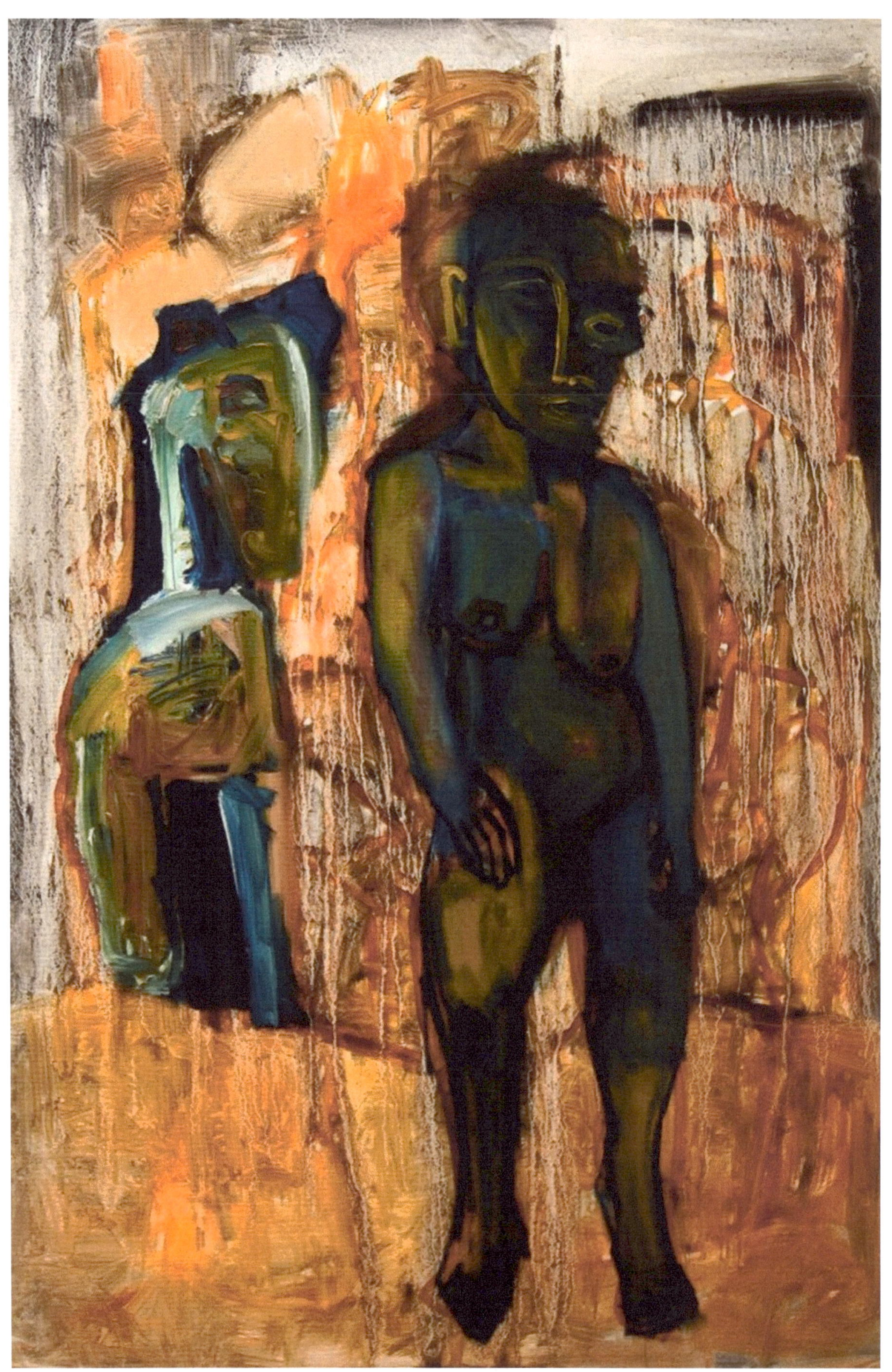

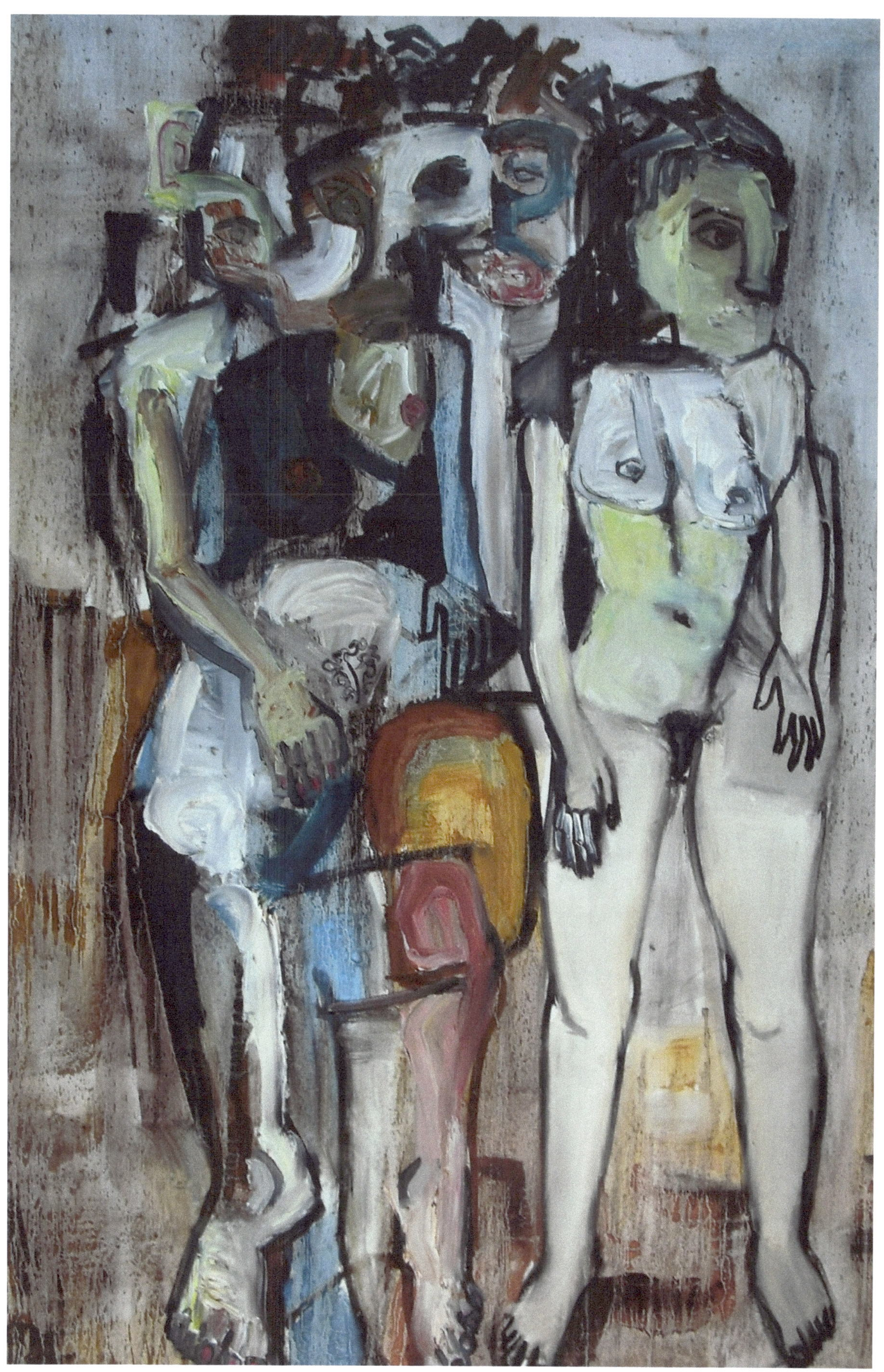

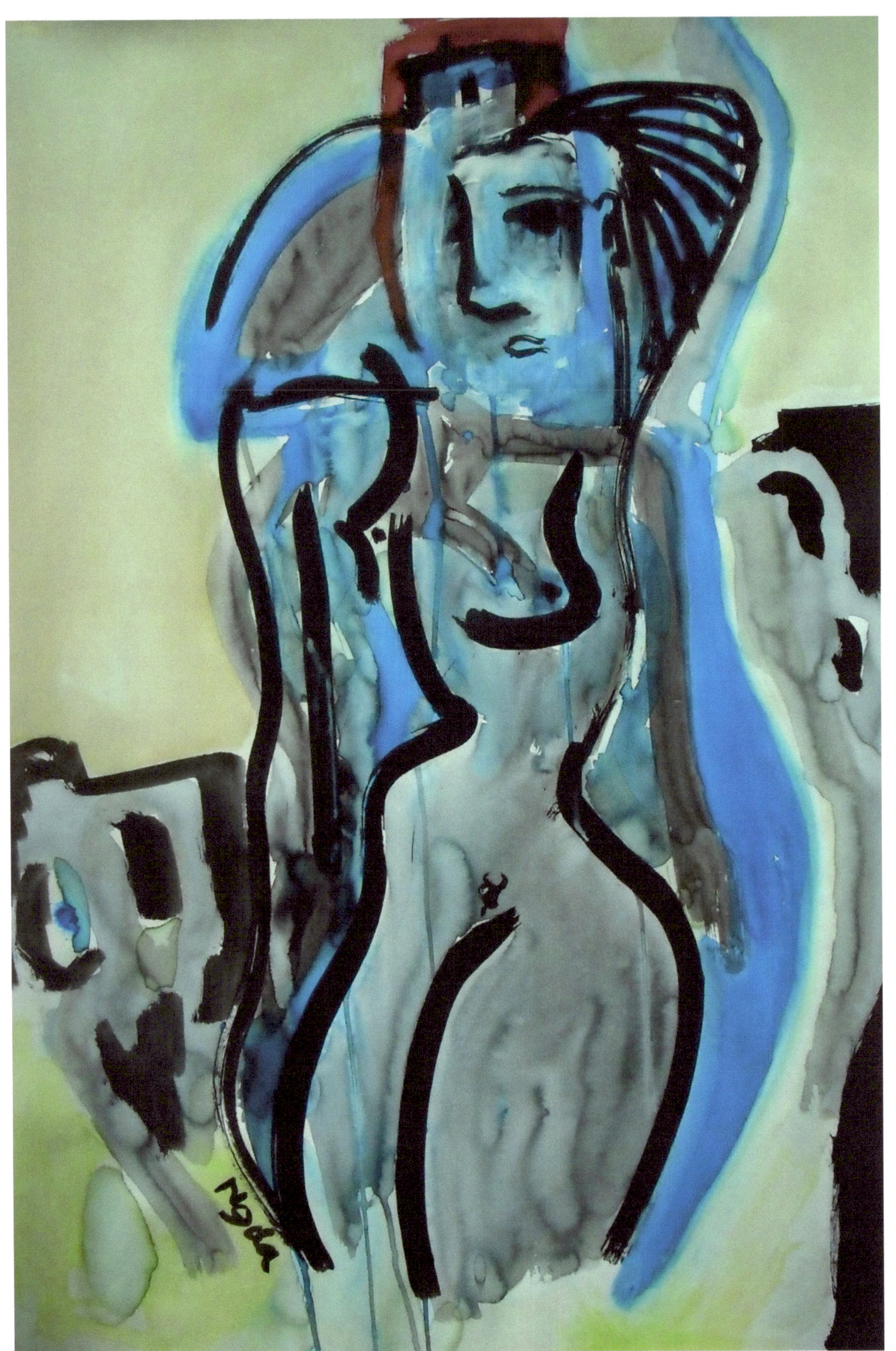

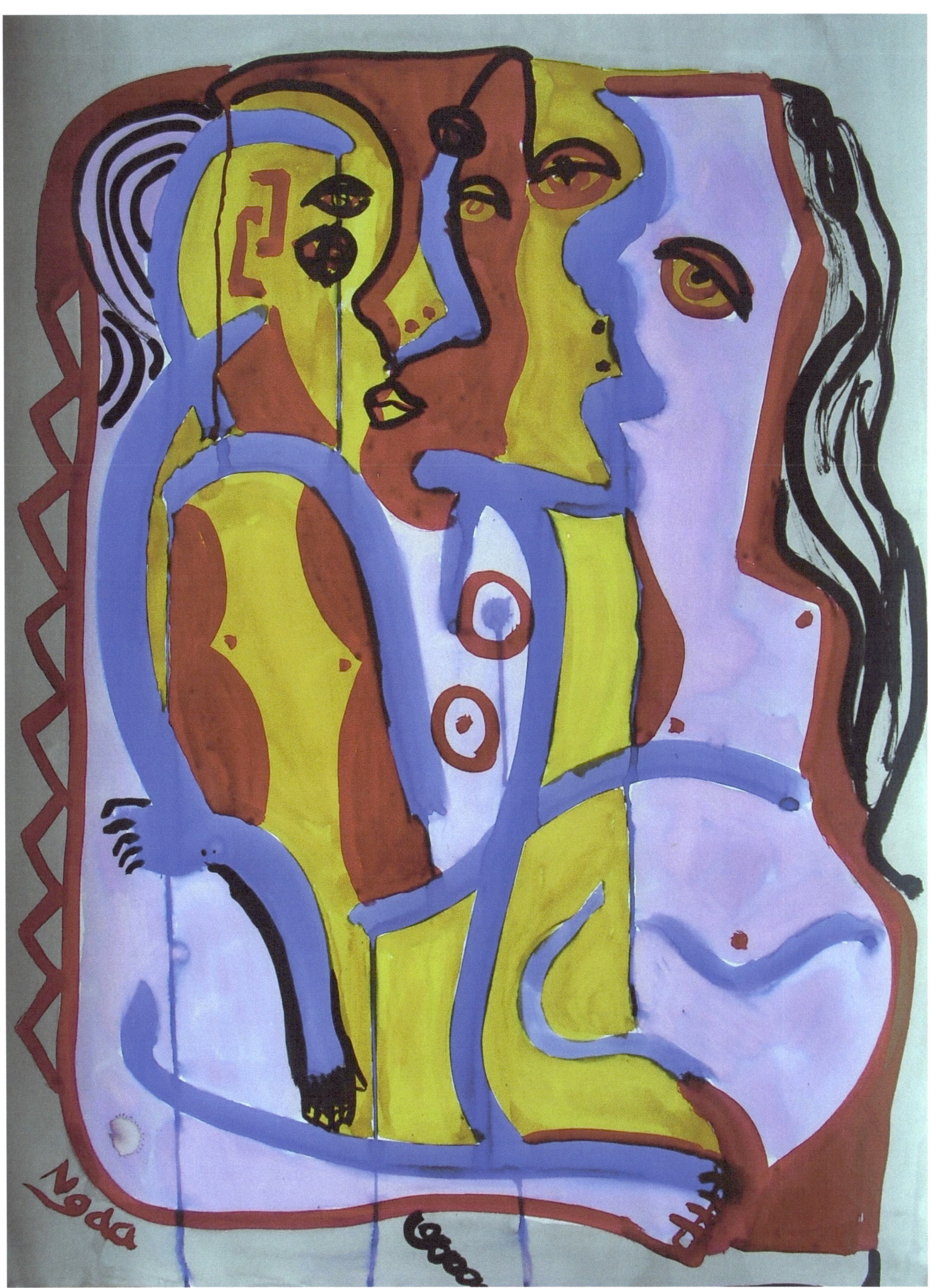

"MOLLY"

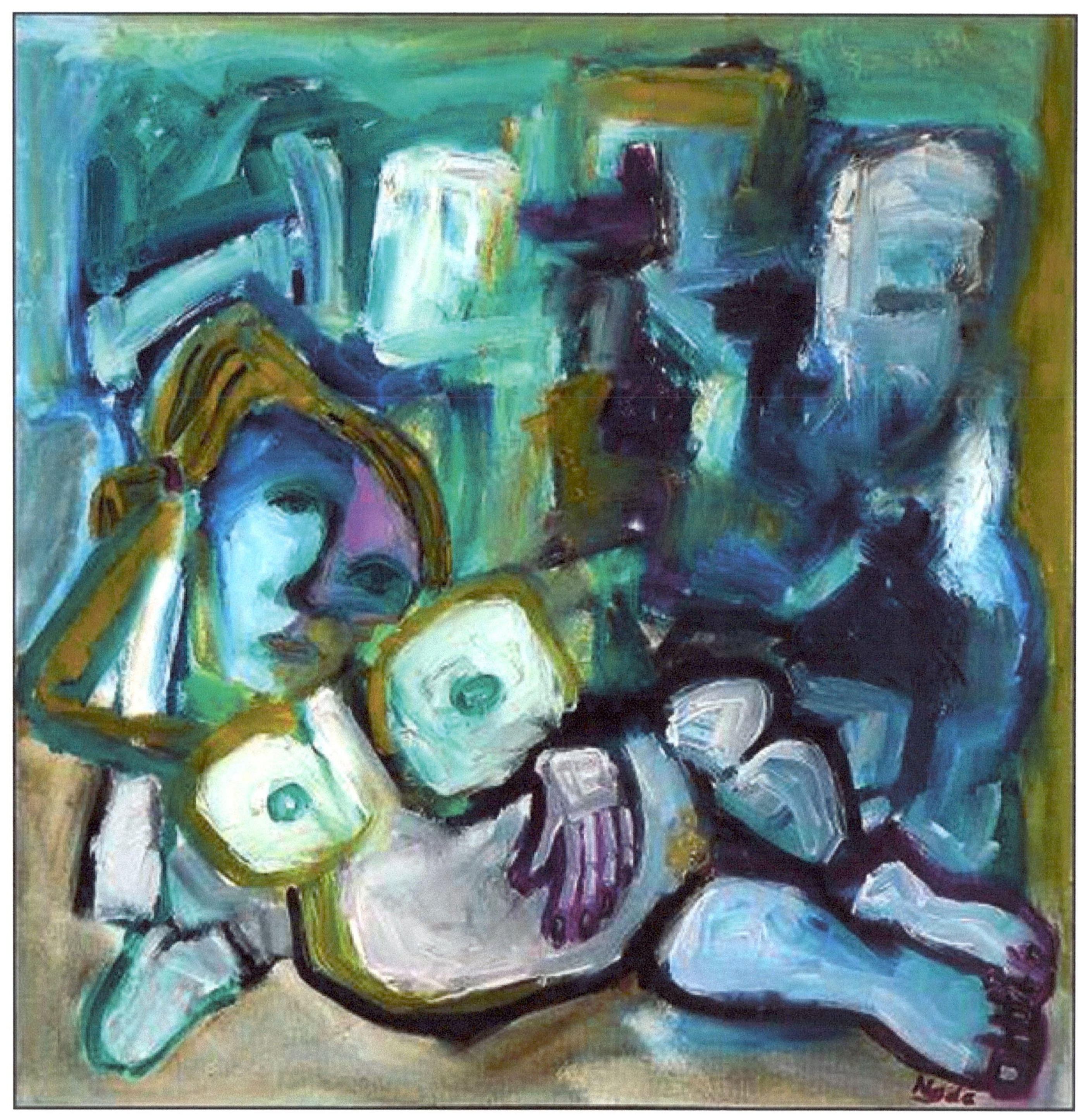

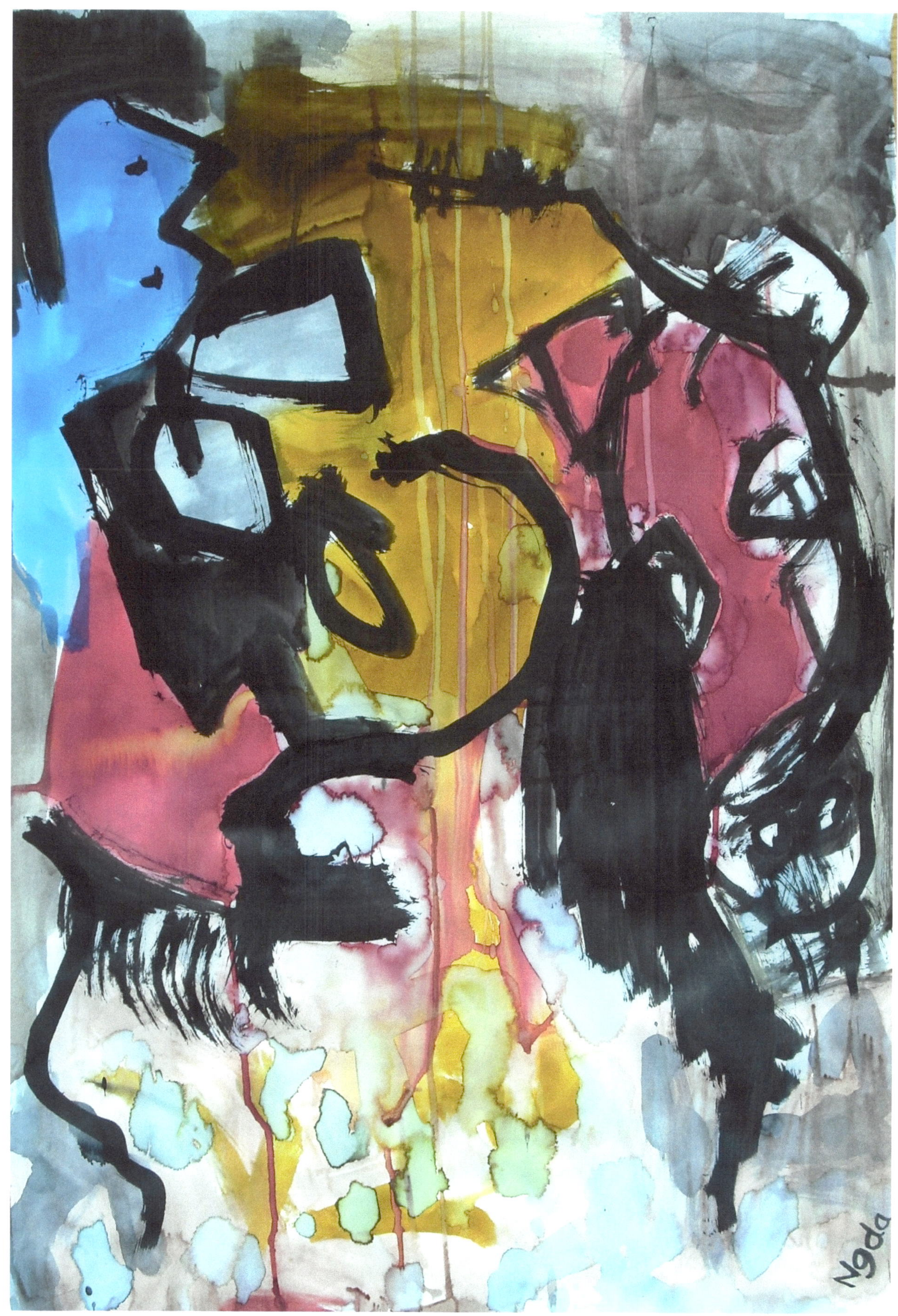

"GIRL AND HORSE"

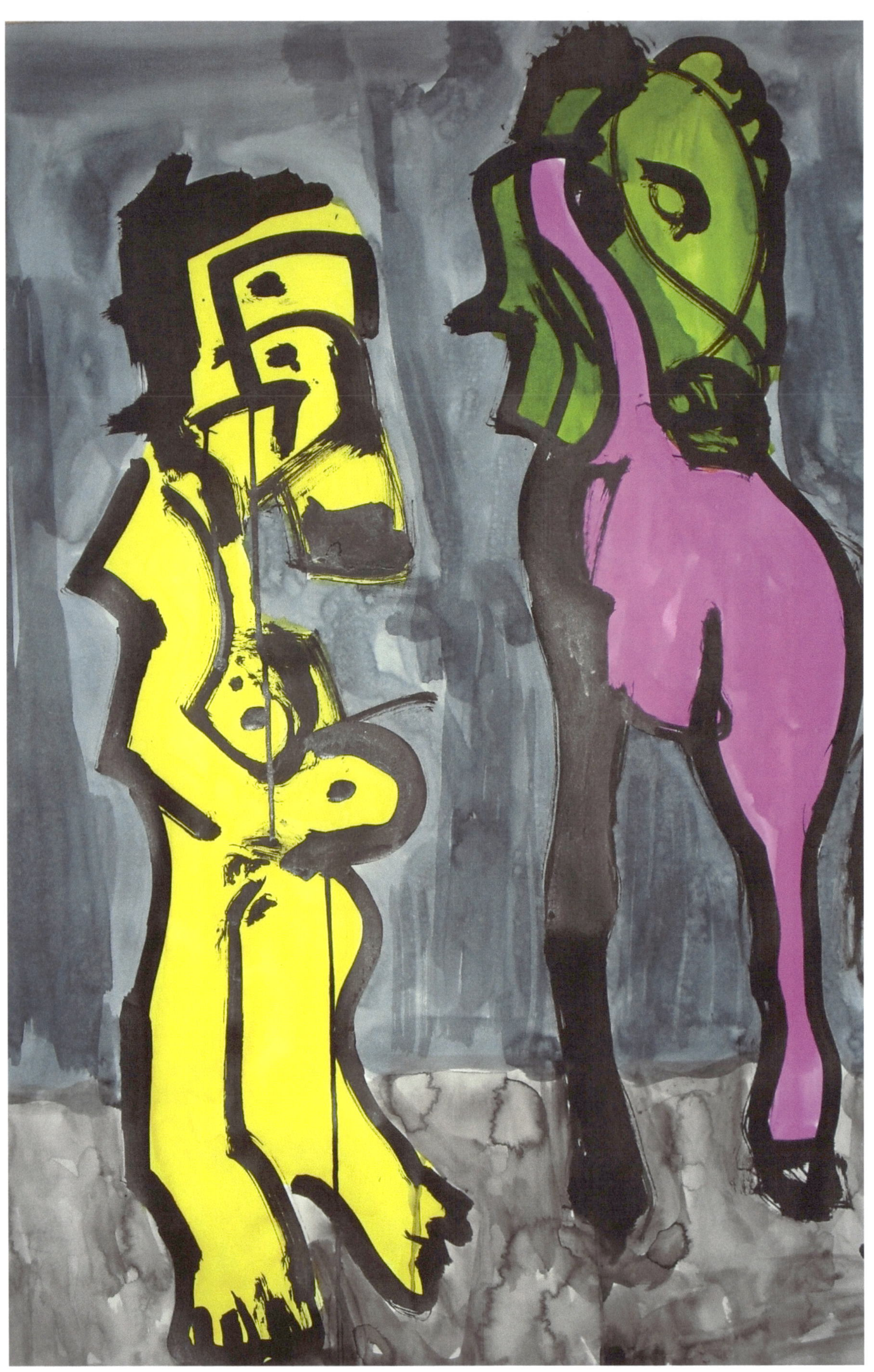

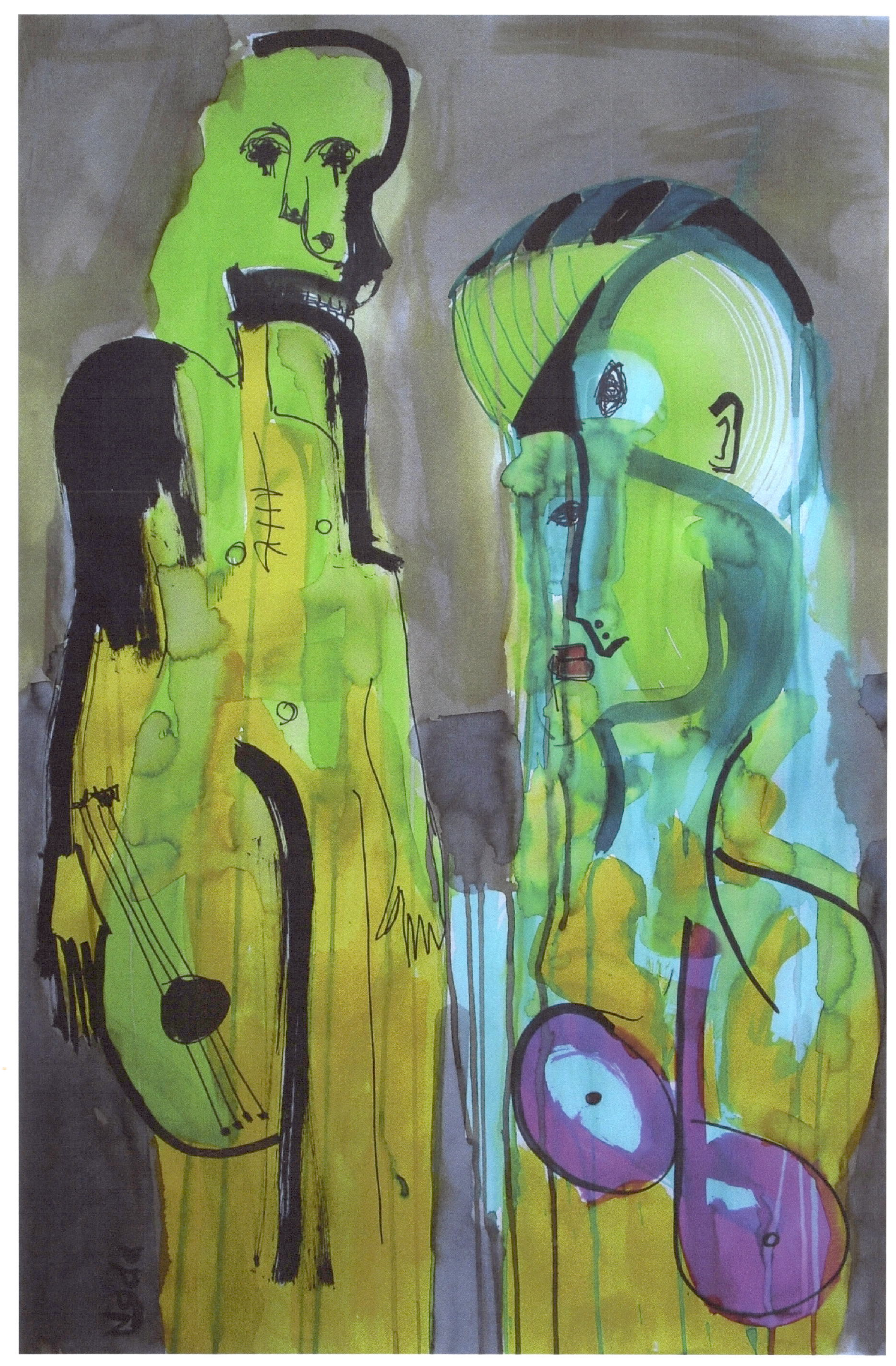

"SHANTI"

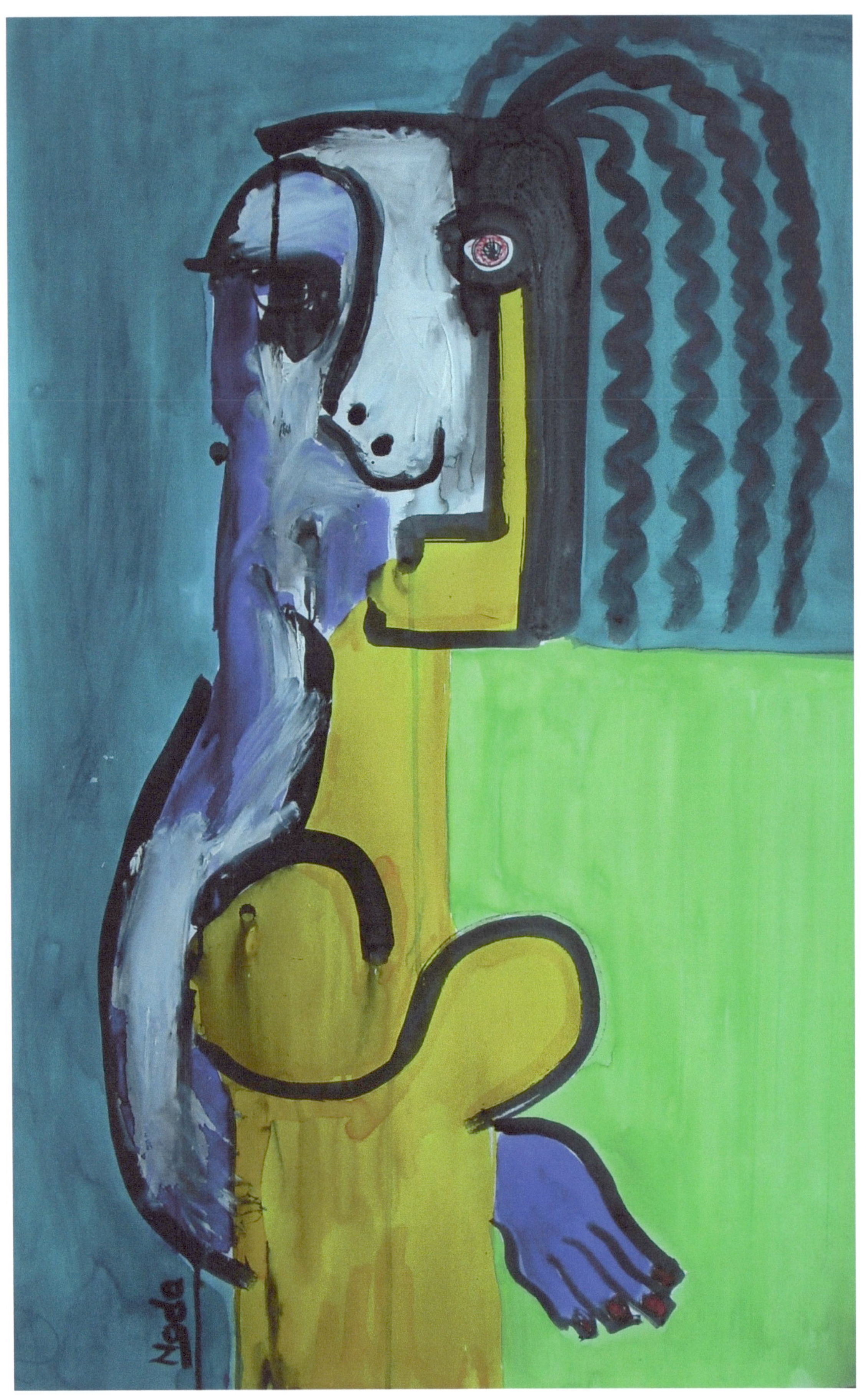

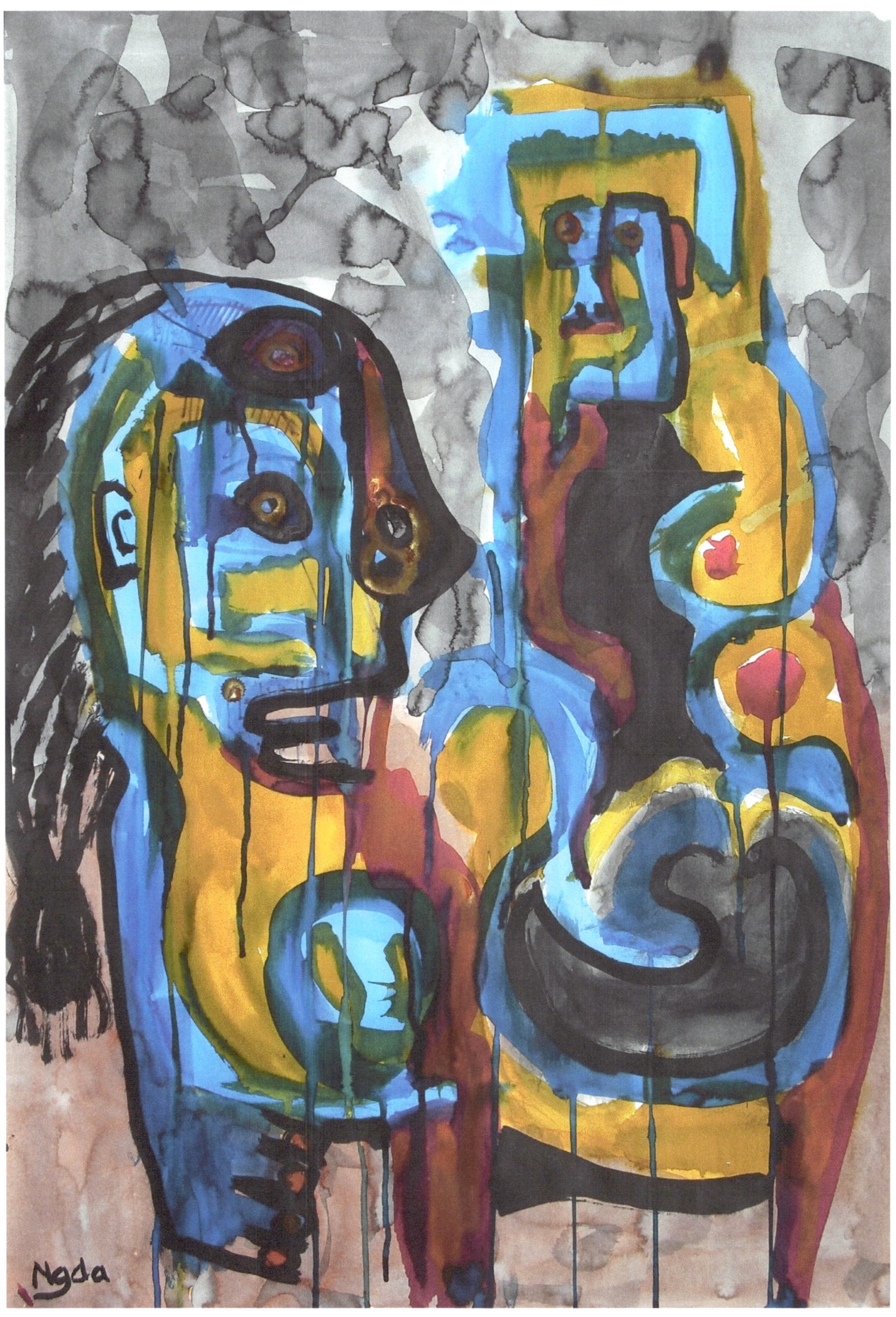

"AMANTES"

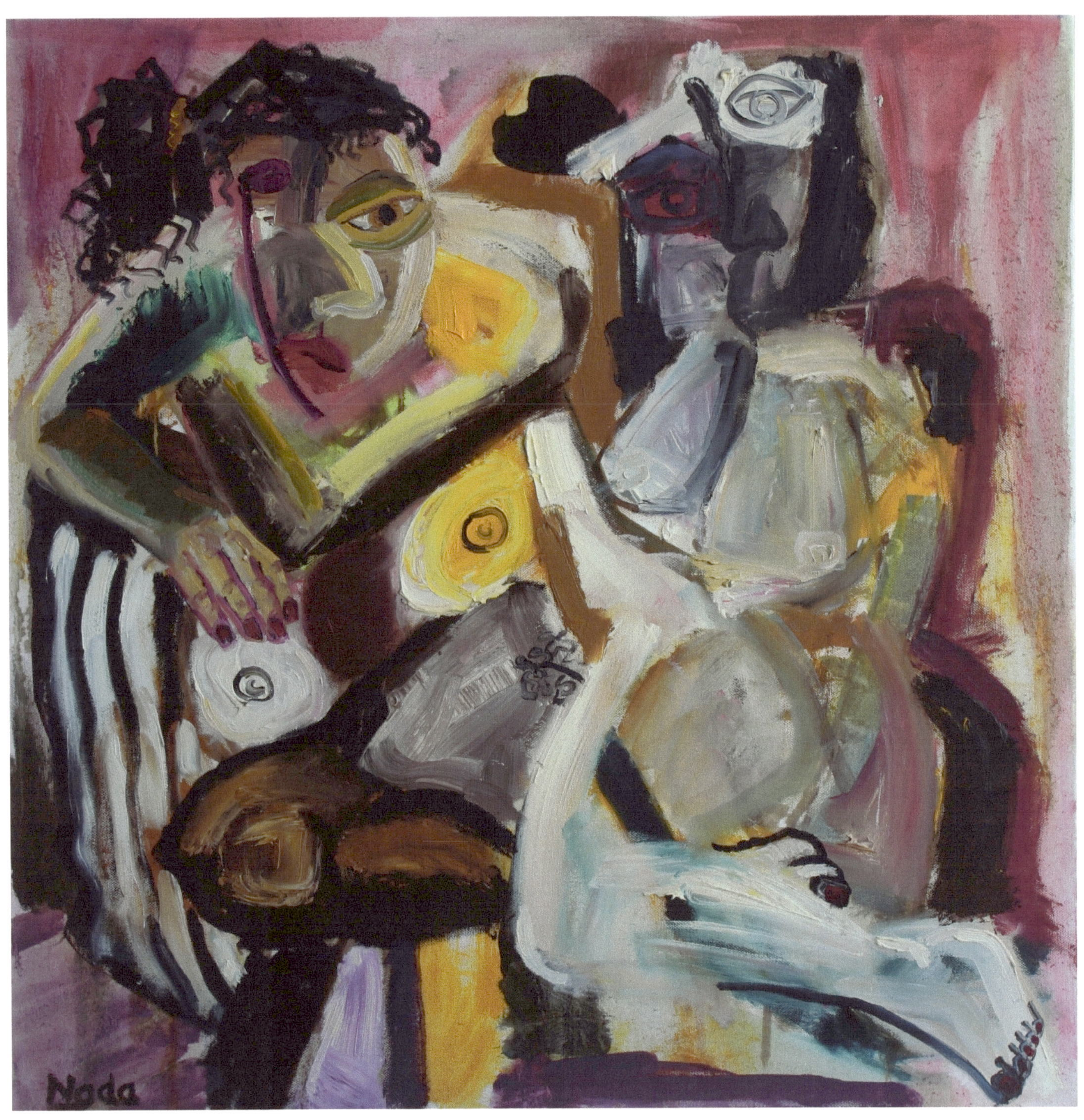

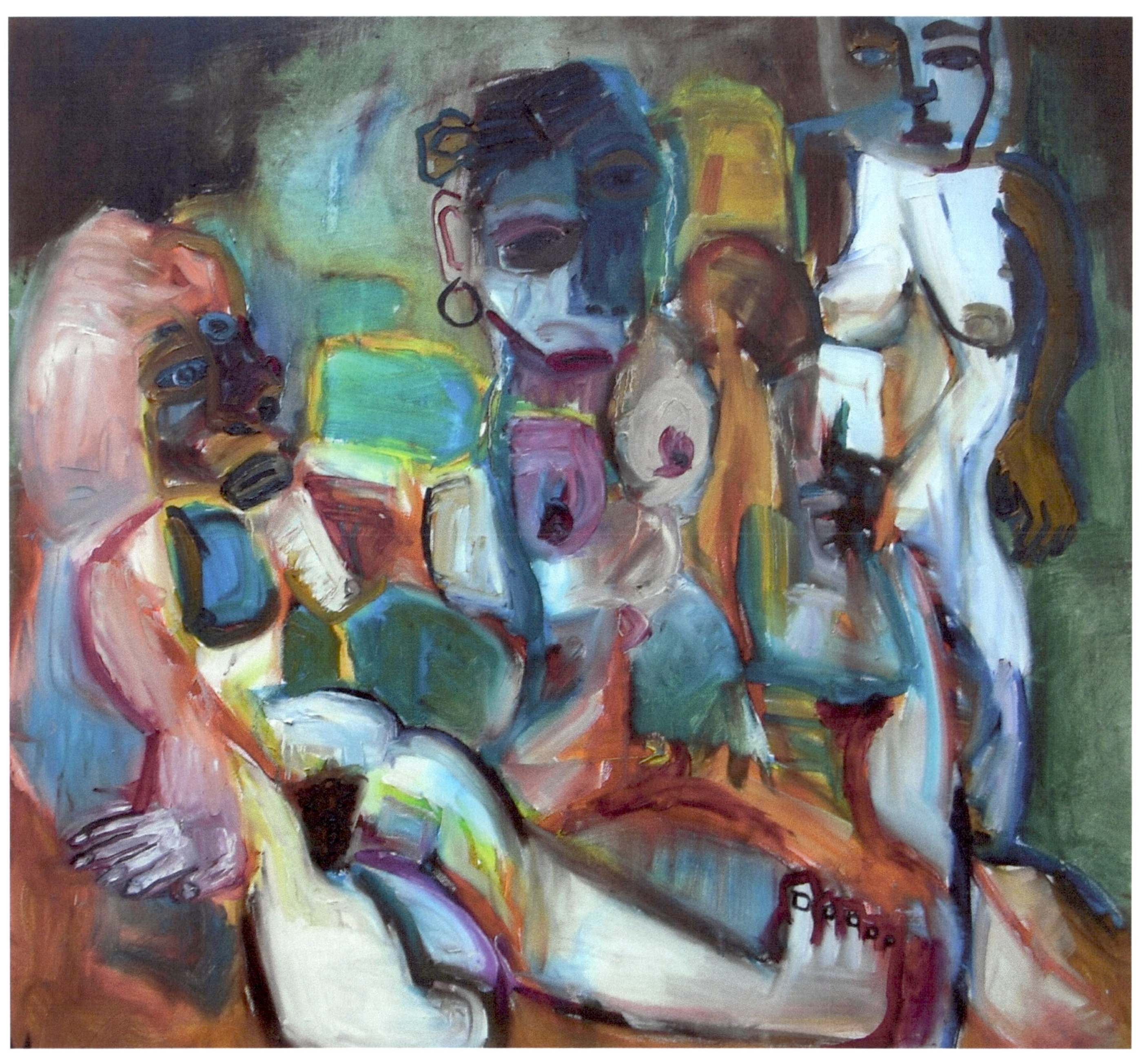

"LE DÉJEUNER SUR L'HERBE (dans l'après-midi)"

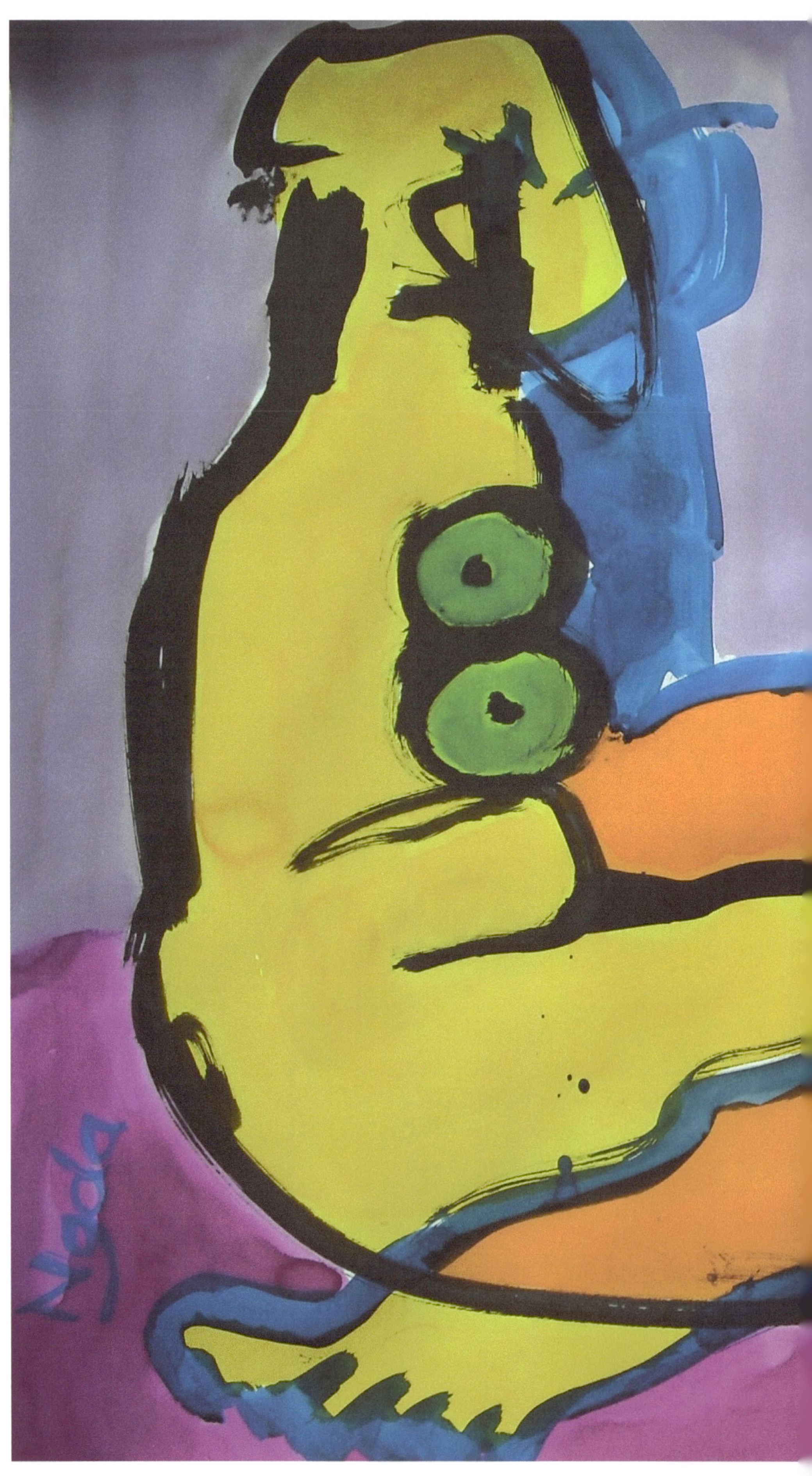

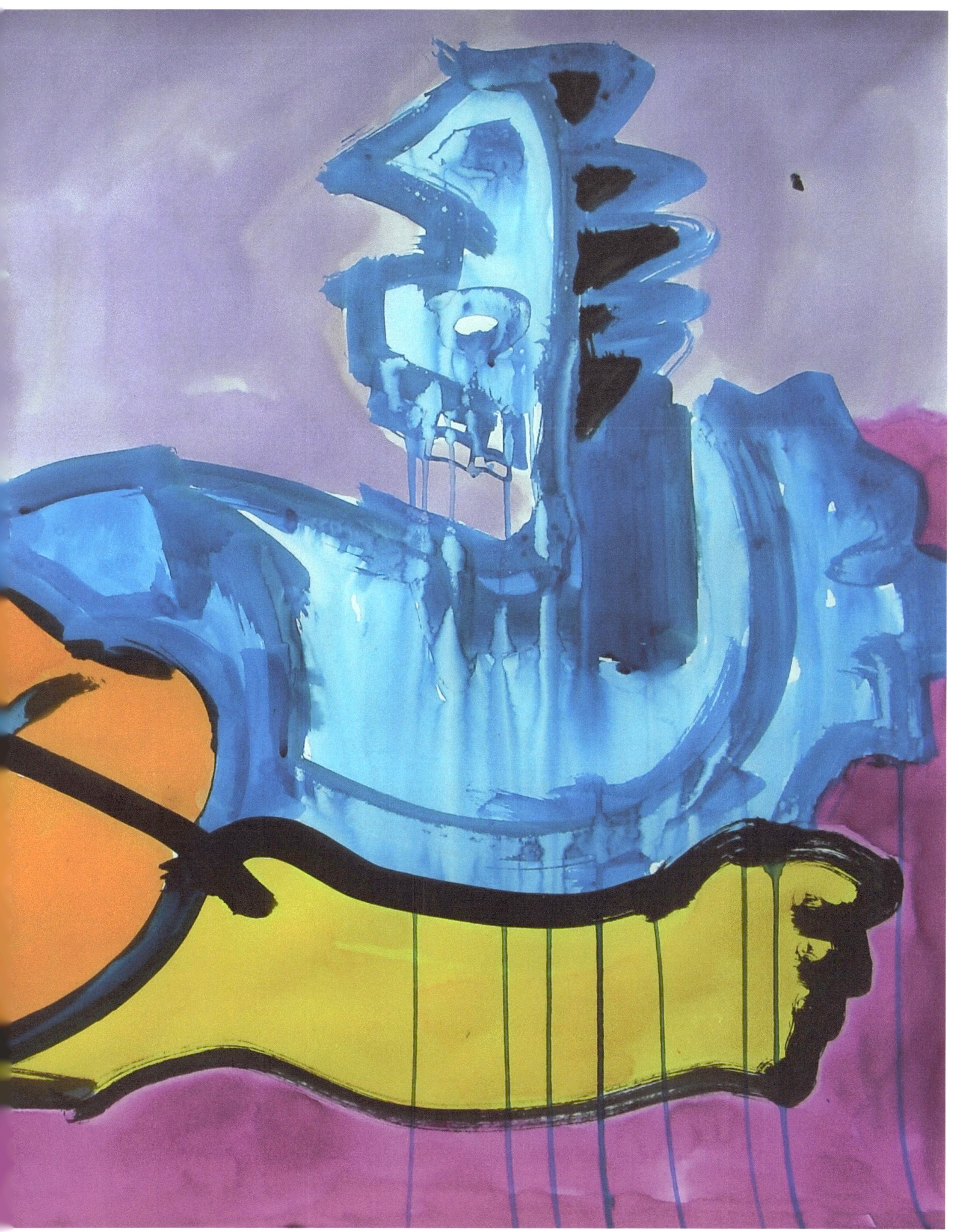

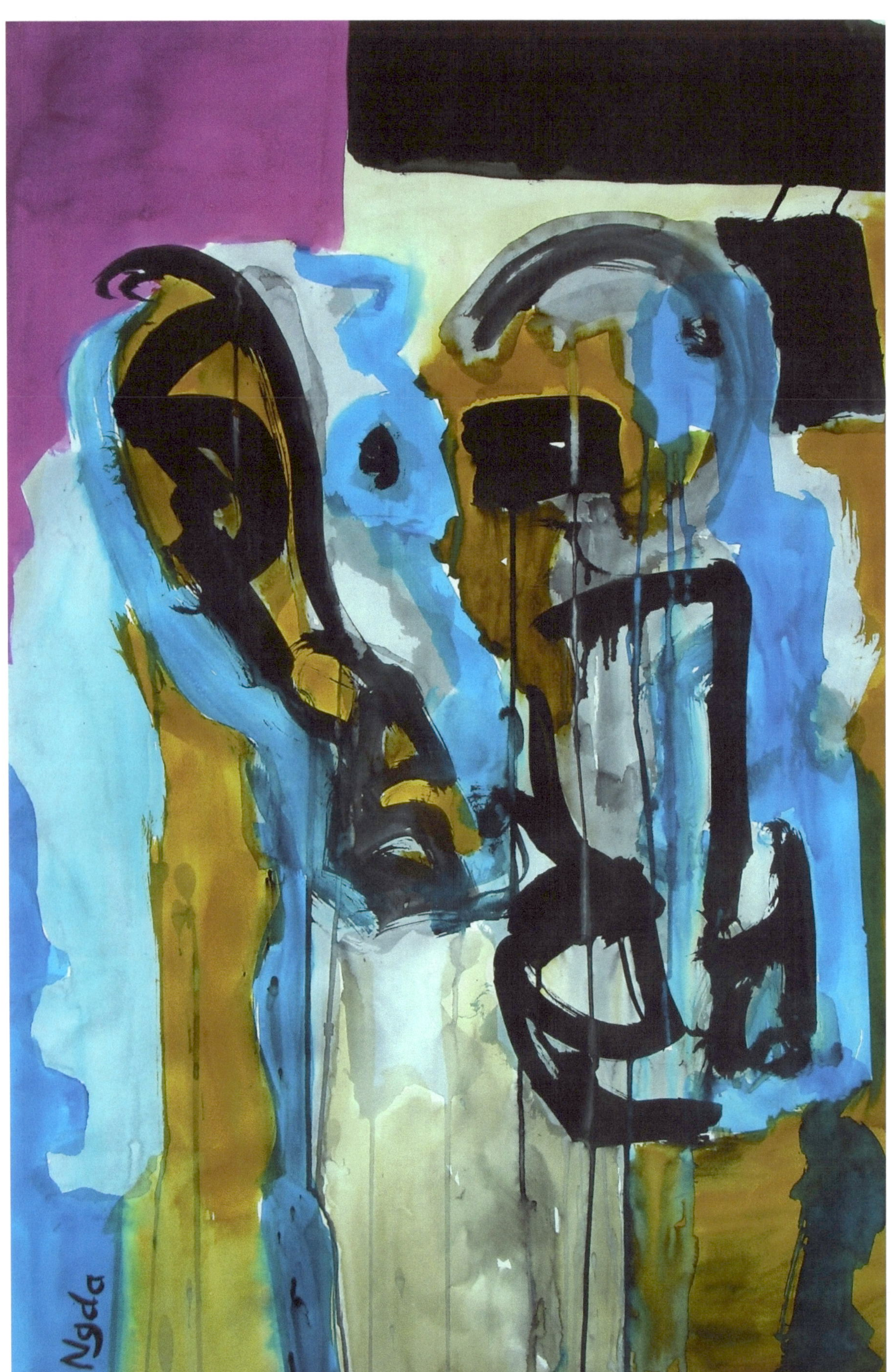

INDEX

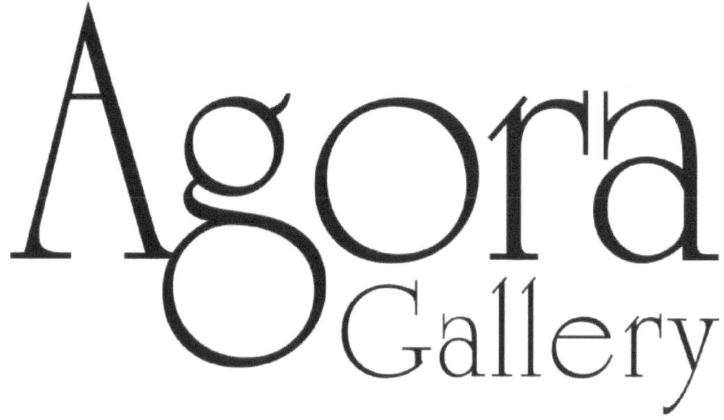

**The artworks were on display at the Agora Gallery
530 W 25th St, Chelsea, New York, USA**

More Artworks by Stephen Najda can be seen:

www.najda.net
Facebook: Najda Art
E-mail enquires: najdaart@gmail.com